Staying the Course: Cultivating Students to Persist to Degree Completion in the Age of College Attrition

Staying the Course: Cultivating Students to Persist to Degree Completion in the Age of College Attrition

A Practical Guide for Student Retention for Policy Makers, School Administrators, Faculty, Parents, and Students

Dr. Abel G. Okagbare, Ed.D.

Copyright © 2017 Dr. Abel G. Okagbare, Ed.D.

All rights reserved. This book or any portion thereof may not be reproduced or used in any manner whatsoever without the express written permission of the publisher except for the use of brief quotations in a book review. First Printing, 2017.

ISBN-13: 9780998965611
ISBN-10: 0998965618

Contents

Introduction · vii
The Student Retention Problem: A National Issue · · · · · · · · ix
What You Will Find in this Book · x

Part One · 1
Student Retention and Student Persistence: Who Stays? · · · · · · · · · · · · · 3
    Traditional College Students · 3
    Issues Facing Special Populations · 9

Part Two · 23
Institutional Characteristics: Which Schools Keep Students? · · · · · · · · 25
    Size of Institution · 26
    Accessibility of Student Services · 26
    Availability of Financial Aid · 28
    Geographic Location · 29
    Ratio of Full-Time to Part-Time Faculty · · · · · · · · · · · · · · · · 30
    Student Retention Programs · 31
    Retention of Students in For-Profit Universities · · · · · · · · · 35
    Big Data Analytics as a Retention Strategy · · · · · · · · · · · · 38

Part Three · 43
Best Practices to Keep Students in School: A Case Study · · · · · · · · · 45
    The For-Profit Institution Model · · · · · · · · · · · · · · · · · · 45
    The Case Study · 47

    Findings from the Thematic Categories · · · · · · · · · · · · · · · 50
    Conclusions · 69

Part Four · **73**
Cultivating the Persistent Student · 75
    The Challenge of Persistence: The Student Perspective · · · · 76
    The Transition to College Life · 77
    Managing Schoolwork · 81
    Student Mental Health · 86

Part Five · **95**
Concluding Remarks and Recommendations for Practice · · · · · · · · · · 97
    Retention in Theory: Key Concepts · · · · · · · · · · · · · · · · · · 99
    Retention in Practice: Recommendations for Institutions · · · 100

    References · 105

Introduction

At a moment when the total student debt load in the United States stands at a staggering 1.2 trillion dollars, questions about job skills, higher education, a dramatic rise in loan defaults, and the ever-increasing cost of going to college have become major political and social issues. Consequently, access to higher education sits at the center of plans to maintain a flexible and skilled workforce that can respond to the changing demands of a technology-based global economy. More abstractly, many view college education as a key part of social mobility in American life, a means by which children born into lower socioeconomic groups can advance into the middle class and beyond.

The benefits of higher education have come at a cost, both literal and figurative; however, much attention has been paid to the dramatic increase in the cost of tuition and the student loan debt associated with it. Some institutions have come under intense scrutiny from both federal regulators and consumers for leaving students with very large debt burdens and few employment prospects. Even when colleges and universities do not make false promises, student loan obligations can force graduates to delay home ownership or starting a family. However, in the United States, a college education is increasingly required in order to obtain employment in occupations that can support a middle-class lifestyle. Unfortunately, it is often noted that despite its increasing cost, a bachelor's degree is now worth, in terms of its earning power, what a high school diploma was worth until this country began its transition from an industrial to a service-based economy. Colleges and universities, both traditional and for-profit, have used this fact to justify the substantial financial and time investment that higher education entails. Creating the necessary elements of support for students of all backgrounds so that they may successfully complete their degrees strengthens both the value proposition of a college education and social mobility within American society.

In fact, in the United States (and indeed, much of the rest of the world), a college education is becoming increasingly essential for employment as well as for creating and maintaining a positive standard of living. Education in general is associated with positive economic and social outcomes (Brand & Xie, 2010; Carnevale, Rose, & Cheah, 2012; Hout, 2012). People with higher levels of education "make more money, live healthier lives, divorce less often, and contribute more to the functioning and civility of their communities than less educated people do" (Hout, 2012, p. 394). Current employment projections reveal that by 2018, 63% of open jobs will require some form of postsecondary education (Carnevale et al., 2012), and a 2011 survey by the Business Roundtable revealed that at least two-thirds of U.S. employers expect their employees to have college degrees.

Although many people imagine a "college education" strictly in terms of a four-year undergraduate or bachelor's degree, the tangible benefits of education extend to other forms of certification as well. Although programs that require less than one year of study do not offer significant economic returns when compared to longer programs, certificates of various sorts can have a positive effect on long-term income, especially in specialized or high-demand industries. On average, for instance, holders of associate's degrees earn at least 20% more than those with only a high school diploma (Carnevale et al., 2012). At the same time, Millennials have begun to bypass college in favor of certification programs such as "coding camps" that teach computer programming and offer not only the accelerated acquisition of in-demand technical skills, but also the prospect of moving through a feeder system that can lead to a concrete and well-paying job with a company that will even reimburse successful employees for the cost of the certificate itself.

With these clear indications of the economic benefits of higher education as well as the positive social effects of greater job security and economic mobility, there are a number of government policies in place to help students—particularly those from underrepresented groups or backgrounds—to attend college. These programs and policies, ranging from Pell grants to federal student loans to the GI Bill, make accessing education much more possible for many people. In addition, for-profit colleges and universities have emerged to expand opportunities for nontraditional students and others who have been underserved by traditional institutions of higher education.

The Student Retention Problem: A National Issue

Even with these supports in place, many students have a hard time completing their programs and graduating within a reasonable timeframe. Today, America is home to 34 million students who began and left college without degrees, and members of this population suffer from high levels of unemployment, a high risk of student debt default, and high likelihood of earning one third or less of what a college graduate can expect to make per year (Nelson, 2014). The problem of student retention has been one of the most important issues facing higher education in the 20th and 21st centuries, with most institutions and government agencies attempting to understand why students drop out, while also attempting to help students remain in school. Several studies have pointed to both student characteristics and institutional characteristics as important to determining which students will persist in school until graduation and which ones will fail.

For example, researchers at the National Commission on Higher Education Attainment (2013) reported that the completion rate at for-profit institutions has declined to 43%. By comparison, the completion rate at public educational institutions stands at 61%, while 72% of students at private non-profit institutions complete their degrees (Rubin, 2013). Although perhaps not as well publicized as the impact of rising tuition and ballooning student debt, attrition rates are of great concern to academic policymakers. A high dropout rate affects the careers of students who were unable to complete their educations, and can also have a serious impact on the image of a school (Yu, DiGangi, Jannasch-Pennell, & Kaprolet, 2010). When their students drop out, schools suffer a considerable loss of tuition, fees, alumni contributions, and networking power (DeBerard, Spielmans, & Julka, 2004).

What You Will Find in this Book

This book is written as a tool to help institutions lower their attrition rates. It presents a thorough discussion of reasons why students leave college before graduation, followed by suggestions for student retention best practices. It is primarily aimed at educational professionals, including college counselors, advisors, and academic affairs officers. However, secondary-school guidance counselors, parents, and even students themselves will find useful information here to help them effectively meet their educational goals.

This book is divided into four major sections. In the first, *Student Retention and Student Attrition: Who Stays?* I discuss the subject of student retention by focusing on the characteristics of at-risk students as opposed to the characteristics of the institutions they attend. Here the reader will find an in-depth discussion of the backgrounds and demographics of those students who are at risk of dropping out of college, as well as those who are not. This section also includes a look at challenges to specific student populations: "traditional" college students, "nontraditional" college students, students in online/distance learning programs, minority students, and students from the Millennial generation.

In the second section, *Institutional Characteristics: Which Colleges Keep Students?* I examine the characteristics of colleges that are more and less successful at retaining students through graduation. In the course of examining institutional features that include universities' ratios of full- to part-time faculty, their financial aid offerings, their student retention programs, and even their use of big-data analytics to retain students, a picture begins to emerge in which student success can be measured not by the services offered by the colleges, but rather by the relationships that colleges succeed in building with and between their students.

This theme of relationships built as opposed to services offered is the leitmotif of this book's third section, *What Works: Best Practices to Keep Students in School*. This chapter is based in large part on my dissertation research at ten campuses of a for-profit private university. Five of these campuses had very high student retention rates, while the other five had very low retention rates. My study included interviews with administrators and faculty members aimed at understanding institutional differences between schools with very different levels of student success. The findings from this study have been distilled here into suggestions for colleges and universities looking to increase student persistence and thus raise retention rates.

The fourth section, *Cultivating the Persistent Student*, addresses a dimension of the attrition problem that is sometimes overlooked: what students can do to empower themselves to avoid becoming statistics. In the course of this section, I examine challenges related to the transition to university life, work-life balance, study habits, self-esteem, motivation, self-efficacy beliefs, and other factors that can influence attrition and retention. My hope is that educators and students alike will make use of my findings in ways that encourage students to take charge of and maximize their educational outcomes. This is followed by the final section, *Concluding Remarks and Recommendations for Practice*, which recaps the issue of student retention and the most important messages of the book.

Part One

Student Retention and Student Persistence: Who Stays?

Traditional College Students

Many of the foundational, classic studies of student retention, and many student retention programs themselves, are aimed at so-called "traditional" college students: young adults between the ages of 18–23 who attend college shortly after high-school graduation. With that in mind, we will begin this section with a look at two particularly influential thinkers, Vincent Tinto and Pierre Bourdieu, whose works are widely cited in discussions of retention and attrition among traditional college students.

Traditional students often face several challenges related to late adolescence as well as the transition from high school to college. The unexpected difficulty of many academic subjects along with a mismatch between student expectations and the realities of academic life cause some students to drop out during their first year. But according to Tinto (1993), academic factors alone cannot explain why students fail to complete their degrees. In fact, Tinto posits that only 20% to 30% of students who leave college do so for academic reasons; by contrast, 70% to 80% of those who fail to finish cite a variety of other factors. Some students may be overwhelmed by the social changes (including living on their own, adjusting to new social environments, and balancing academic expectations with other life obligations) and leave school. Some students have difficulty deciding on a major or career path and this, in combination with difficulty navigating social challenges, may cause them to drop out of school.

Some students who have difficulty succeeding in college do not have the sufficient preparation for higher education before and during the admissions process. Others seem to stop engaging with college shortly after entry. Tinto (1993) noted that students' experiences immediately after admission are more important to their ultimate success than interactions before admissions. Students are likely to drop out when they receive little support from the school or when they feel alienated from the college community, and, as we shall see later, school support means little if it cannot mitigate the alienation many students, especially new ones, often feel. All of these factors, in turn, may be compounded by financial issues if students cannot afford the direct and indirect costs of college. Minorities and first-generation students are particularly vulnerable to this sort of alienation and inadequate support from the college, especially if they find academic culture to be very different from their native cultures.

Tinto (1993) further emphasized that the social and academic environment to which students become accustomed will shape their commitment to that educational institution. If students do not manage to integrate their school's value system into their own culture and understanding, they will not be committed to the goal of graduation from that institution. If there is a misalignment between the interests of the student and the mission of the school or the student's program, the student may feel encouraged to leave. In particular, when students feel isolated and do not interact well with other students or faculty, they are more likely to drop out. Tinto's work, based on research by Pascarella, Duby, & Iverson, 1983, as well as that of subsequent scholars using his model, noted that persistence in college is heavily influenced by two major factors: structural integration and normative integration. Structural integration provides students with the extrinsic rewards necessary to continue in the pursuit of an education, whereas normative integration looks at the intrinsic rewards of intellectual improvement. The presence of both factors was a significant predictor for students' continuance in higher education (Pascarella et al., 1983), and so the students who succeed are often those who are open or ready, for whatever reason, to respond to these modes of integration.

Bourdieu's work on student retention focuses on how financial capital, human capital, cultural capital, and social capital affect student retention. In an educational context, financial capital includes students' exposure to money, income, assets, and expenses. Likewise, in the university setting, human capital is measured by the level of education attained through degrees, certificates, and diplomas; awards and honors earned; training experiences; and job history. Cultural capital includes the collection of noneconomic assets such as family background, values, social class, varying investments in and commitments to education, different resources, and any advantages an individual has which gives him a higher status in society. Like high expectations, cultural capital is generally provided by parents to their children. Finally, social capital includes the resources based on personal relationships, group memberships, and networks of influence and support. Education is a measure of human capital but it also relates to financial capital because better employment opportunities come with greater education.

Within the framework of Bourdieu (1986), the classifications of capital are convertible from one type to another. For example, economic capital may translate to higher social capital and higher human capital, and vice versa, thus increasing the correlations among these factors. These broad categories of capital when operationalized take many forms in the research literature: (a) background and defining variables investigated because of the generally accepted premise that past behavior is expected to predict future behavior, (b) barriers in the persistence for completion of an undergraduate degree or in other words, causes for dropout, and (c) environmental variables or factors which the student or the institution has little or extremely limited control over (Bean & Metzner, 1985).

Of these four kinds of capital, social capital seems to be particularly important in the college setting, and scholars studying it have found unexpected links between institutional characteristics and student demographics. In a study of 346 students at a large research university, Beattie and Thiele (2016) used the concept of academic social capital to describe academic interactions, and discovered novel connections between class size and educational outcomes for Black and Latino students, who reported having significantly fewer academic interactions with faculty than white students. Because of the limited interactions allowed in large classes, these classes are conduits for less academic social capital than small ones. The authors noted that programs designed to welcome and assimilate minority students may be misguided given the importance of the more meaningful academic social interaction made possible by small classes. When academic social relationships become limited by class size, those students entering college with the least academic social capital are vulnerable to adverse educational outcomes. In the work of Beattie and Thiele, we can see again that substantial relationships between students and faculty, and between students, can be better pathways to persistence than those promised by certain non-academic services designed to increase socialization and in that way to prevent attrition. Indeed, we shall see later why such well-intentioned programs often do not have the intended effect of increasing student persistence.

Scholars have also arrived at striking conclusions when studying attrition with reference to Bourdieu's concept of *habitus*. A habitus can be thought of as a culturally- and socially-created mental framework consisting of sensibilities, dispositions, and preferences that we deploy when interacting within a social environment. An internal habitus is established by the cultural and social structures we are accustomed to and identify with, and, importantly, it can determine what we conceive of as attainable or possible in life when we move into social circumstances different from the habitus we have been exposed to and internalized.

Using this concept of habitus as a touchstone, Lehmann (2007) investigated the relationships between attrition and the social/class status of students. Through interviews within a qualitative study of several dozen dropouts from a large research university, Lehmann found that first-generation students are likely to drop out even when they are performing well academically. Such students have reported that they felt unable to fit in or to relate to other students, or to "feel the university." And so in this case, new students dropped out due to the discontinuity between their acquired habitus and the new one they found themselves within.

Other scholars (e.g., Paulsen & St. John, 2002) have linked the concept of habitus to the idea of a "financial nexus between college choice and persistence decisions," wherein,

One's habitus would operate implicitly to frame, constrain, and inform the patterns of students' responses to financial factors in such choices in ways that are consistent with the views of others in the student's social class. In other words, each student's habitus serves to "situate" or "contextualize" their choices, and it represents a set of relatively stable predispositions with respect to what the student will see and value regarding the financial aspects of choice and persistence decisions. (Paulsen & St. John, 2002)

This sociocultural model of how new students view their college costs revealed some surprising things. For instance, in this study, the availability of financial aid and work-study were not predictors of retention among poor or working-class students, but rather predictors instead of "the reproduction of social class" within the educational system. These same students are also equipped with a financial habitus that affects their perception of tuition increases to such an extent that, for poor students, every $1,000 increase in tuition increased the risk of dropout by 16% to 19% (Paulsen & St. John, 2002). But in this case, it was not the actual affordability of college, but rather the way its costs are filtered through the financial habitus of its poorer students, that had the most significant effects on attrition. The main point here is, again, that a student's acquired habitus has the potential to affect his or her ability to fit into a new one, whether in financial terms, or in more socio-cultural ones.

Institutional and individual factors interact in complex ways to affect persistence, and research has shown that certain characteristics of both schools and individual students affect retention rates (Bowden & Wood, 2011; Ceci, Williams, & Barnett, 2009; England, 2010; Sontam & Gabriel, 2012). Almost 50% of students enrolled in community colleges throughout the country drop out before they earn their diplomas (Windham, Rehfuss, Williams, Pugh, & Tincher-Ladner, 2014), but some students are more vulnerable than others. Interestingly, factors like race and socioeconomic status are not as important as a student's score on the

Reading portion of the ACT COMPASS, a computer-adaptive college placement test (Windham et al., 2014). In addition, student engagement with activities and attitude toward schoolwork have been shown to be generally more significant than factors like ethnicity on retention, language, income, and gender. Perhaps unsurprisingly, Veenstra (2009) found that the first year of college is often the most important in terms of the decision to drop out or stay in school.

Socioeconomic status in particular has a complex relationship to student retention. Although one study found that students from lower-income families were more likely to drop out of college than those from wealthier backgrounds (Arendt, 2013), another found no difference in college completion rates between students from lower- and middle-income backgrounds, although upper-income students were still more likely to graduate than their lower- or middle-income counterparts (Dwyer, Hodson, & McCloud, 2013). One explanation of this finding may be that lower-income families do not necessarily consider college to be a normative adolescent experience, so lower-income students are actually a select group of unusually highly motivated people for whom college was a personal decision. This increased motivation may offset some of the effects of limited financial resources in the same way that access to greater financial resources may help wealthier students persist even when individual motivation may be lacking (Dwyer et al., 2013).

When examining which students are more likely to finish their post-secondary education, it is also important to look at the resources that they had access to in high school. The economic composition of high schools can be a factor in the rate at which students who enroll in a college within the calendar year of high-school graduation will drop out (Niu & Tienda, 2013), with students who graduated from wealthy high schools being more likely to persist in college. Along with the financial resources that most graduates of wealthy high schools carry with them, students at these high schools often receive more preparation for college in the form of college orientations, advanced-placement classes, and family expectations.

Furthermore, for students pursuing a degree during the "traditional" college years, parents and their satisfaction with the school may play a key role in student retention. If parents feel that the school meets their expectations, they will have confidence in the institution and not feel the need to be involved (Sgro, 2006). However, if parents believe that the school is not meeting their expectations, they may pressure their children to drop out or transfer, or they may directly remove their children from the institution. One major factor that parents use to determine satisfaction with a college or university is the quality of faculty and general academic rigor (Walters & McCay, 2005). Parents are especially interested in faculty care and concern for students, faculty subject matter expertise, and overall academic rigor. Parents also look at factors like social environment, character-building opportunities, and the particular educational offerings of the school in deciding whether to stay or leave.

Student learning outcomes can be measured in a number of different ways. A study by Hu, McCormick, and Gonyea (2012) showed that student GPAs were the best predictor of persistence in college, followed by measures of self-reported gains. Direct-assessment learning gains were the least likely to explain persistence (Hu, McCormick, & Gonyea, 2012), although student engagement did emerge as an important factor.

Issues Facing Special Populations

Up to this point, we have been examining the attributes and experiences of majority-typical college students who enter college immediately after high school and who are demographically average as compared to the overall population of U.S. colleges and universities. However, certain groups of students face particular challenges to their ability to complete their programs. For-profit universities, who tend to serve student populations that are from a variety of backgrounds and more likely to be minority, older, and/or engaged in online or distance learning, it is particularly important to examine ways to help specific groups of students persist in their education.

Nontraditional students. Many of the same factors that apply to traditional college students also apply to students who matriculate later in life. However, students entering school after the age of 25 often face additional challenges, such as navigating careers, dependent children, and other life obligations. Considering that many students at for-profit universities are female heads-of-households, helping nontraditional students to balance their academic, professional, and life responsibilities is crucial for maintaining student retention rates.

Like many of the students who attend them, for-profit colleges can also be described as "nontraditional." More than two million students are enrolled in for-profit universities in the United States (Cellini & Goldin, 2012), and a large majority of students in for-profit universities are adults who want to pursue higher education within a flexible and convenient context (Lansing & Olsen, 2011; Sibson, Gregory, & Kurisky, 2014). The popularity and resilience of for-profit universities has been attributed to the flexibility of the business model to expand and adapt to the changes in the needs of students in their pursuit of higher education (Sladek, 2014; Yu & Ertl, 2014). However, many students who enroll in for-profit universities such as those offering online courses drop out after the first two courses, suggesting that the decision to enroll may be motivated by exploratory reasons only (Boston, Ice, & Gibson, 2011). For-profit universities tend to have lower retention rates in the first year compared to traditional colleges (Willcoxson, Cotter, & Joy, 2011).

Although we may think of nontraditional students as those who delay entry into college, the National Center for Education Statistics (NCES) indicated in 2002 that when we broaden the definition of "nontraditional" to include the following criteria, up to 75% of all students may fall into that same category:

- entry to college delayed by at least one year following high school,
- having dependents,
- being a single parent,
- being employed full time,

- being financially independent,
- attending part time, and
- not having a high school diploma. (Ross-Gordon, 2011)

As we shall see in Part 3, for-profit colleges are especially attractive to nontraditional students because such colleges offer students flexible scheduling, distance education, accelerated learning, and individualized programs of study. These offerings are among the reasons why in 2013, a full 70% of full-time students older than 24, and 78% of part-time students in the same age group, chose to attend private, for-profit colleges and universities.

Although attrition rates overall tend to be higher in the for-profit educational sector than in the non-profit sector, nontraditional students also face persistence challenges unique to their demographic. Studies have shown that off-campus nontraditional students who work may be especially at risk because they can fall into a vicious cycle in which job security and educational dedication become two agents in a zero-sum game (Gilardi & Guglielmetti, 2011). These same authors also pointed out that the relative autonomy and independence of adult learners may make them feel that it is unnecessary to accrue the kind of academic social capital that comes from engagement in academic interactions.

Finally, the nontraditional students at greatest risk of failure or attrition are those who fall into more as opposed to fewer of the categories listed above (Pusser et al., 2007). Additionally, students who choose to be educated in programs far outside the educational mainstream—such as non-certificate programs or employer training—tend to be at the highest risk of attrition. This is just to say that the more nontraditional an educational program is, the more at risk for attrition its students will be.

Gender groups. The experiences of male and female college students can be different, and these differences can be reflected in the institutional support received, the programs pursued, and educational outcomes (Fox, Sonnert, & Nikiforova, 2011; Sontam & Gabriel, 2012). However, both male and female college students are expected to benefit from pursing and completing college education (Brand & Xie, 2010). For both genders, education is associated with increased salary and higher levels of community functioning (Hout, 2012).

As early as the 1960s, the relationship of gender and ethnicity with retention had already been studied, but with mixed and inconclusive results. Several studies found that the attrition rate for men is lower than for women (Bowen & Rudenstine, 1992; Lemp, 1980; Zwick, 1991). Other research has suggested that faculty members are more supportive of students of their own gender, particularly males. Presley's (1996) study found that women are more likely to complete their degrees and generally are more satisfied and achieved higher grades. However, other studies (Bair, 1999) found gender to be insignificant in predicting completion of a doctoral degree. Kolb (2005) stated that gender has always been included in the retention studies, which identified that women tend to persist at higher education than men. Three separate studies undertaken in 2006 all found that women were more likely to graduate than men, and, more dramatically, the work of DesJardin, Kim, and Rzonca (2003) concluded that the female dropout rate is higher than males' by about 1.6 times. However, studies do exist that have found no correlation between gender and retention, so more work needs to be done to if we are going to have a precise understanding of this issue.

If we turn to the question of gender and debt, we find that both male and female college students who take out loans generally have the same amount of debt in college, with an average total of $30,100 upon graduation (Lobosco, 2016). However, female students are more likely than male students to take out educational loans. The higher tendency for female students to take loans for their college education can be explained by the perception that women need college degrees to acquire decent jobs (England, 2010).

If female students do indeed take on more educational debt than males, especially in for-profit colleges, they are on the cutting edge of a national tendency. In a study by Belfield (2013), the student loans and repayment rates of students in the specific context of for-profit colleges were analyzed. The author found that students in private for-profit colleges borrow money at a rate four times higher than students enrolled in public colleges. Moreover, repayment of loans is likely to be lower from students enrolled in for-profit colleges compared to students from public colleges. This study showed how paying a tuition fee can be more difficult to sustain for the entire program for students enrolled in for-profit colleges, possibly affecting retention. And, if indeed female students are more likely than males to drop out of college, their financial situations will be affected by the lack of degree combined with a large debt burden.

But interestingly, even though female students take on more debt than men do, male students are more likely than females to drop out from college as a result of debt (Dwyer et al., 2013). The implication here is that debt is a more significant barrier for program completion among male college students than it is for female college students. Because of the relatively lower pay of women in the workforce compared to men, female students tend to value a college diploma more than their male counterparts do (England, 2010).

Other studies have analyzed whether or not male and female students differ in terms of antecedents of institutional loyalty such as satisfaction, trust, and commitment. In addressing the challenges of student attrition, Bowden and Wood (2011) analyzed, based on a sample of 447 students, the results of a structural equation that indicated no significant difference in the satisfaction, trust, and commitment of male and female students. Moreover, both male and female students seek psychological attachment to their institutions, and that student satisfaction can motivate students to be more loyal to their college or university. However, engagement tends to be higher among female students compared to male students (Sontam & Gabriel, 2012).

The nature and type of college curricula may also influence gender difference in terms of attrition (Ackerman, Kanfer, & Beier, 2013; Ceci et al., 2009; Eddy, Brownell, & Wenderoth, 2014). In science, technology, engineering, and mathematics (STEM) programs, the number of male students who complete them tends to be higher as compared to female students (Ackerman et al., 2013). And, perhaps controversially, a meta-analytic review conducted by Ceci et al. (2009) attributed this male/female STEM completion difference to content abilities, with male students usually excelling more in spatial abilities and mechanical knowledge when compared to female students. Moreover, STEM programs tend to be dominated by male students, with female students generally underrepresented (Eddy et al., 2014) except in undergraduate programs in biology wherein 60% are female students (Amelink, 2009).

However, women have made considerable progress in attending and completing college courses. Females now generally perform better than males on several educational benchmarks such as college-going rates, enrollment persistence, graduation rates, and admission to graduate programs (DiPrete & Buchmann, 2006). In addition, over half of undergraduate enrollments are now women.

Minority students. Although as stated above, race is not necessarily an accurate predictor of whether a student will finish college, the rates of completion and attrition across different racial and ethnic groups does differ significantly. More specifically, white students are more likely to graduate from programs that they enroll in than African-American or Latino students. This may be because of various social, emotional, and academic factors (Branson et al., 2013). Unraveling these factors is vital to maintaining high student retention rates, especially at for-profit colleges and universities, which tend to have higher proportions of minority students than traditional public colleges and universities.

Summerskill (1962) noted a correlation between ethnicity and college dropout rates. The dropout rate is highest for African-American students (30.1%), followed by Latinos (29.2%), whites, (18.8%) and finally Asian students (14.9%) (Kezar & Eckel, 2007). Some of this difference may be attributed to socioeconomic factors, since minority students often come from lower-income backgrounds. Many institutions attempt to bridge this gap in completion rates with special diversity initiatives such as scholarships or clubs for students of color and resident-life programs offering housing and activities that emphasize diversity. However, these efforts often lack coordination and result in a limited impact on minority dropout rates.

Using a phenomenological approach, Foster (2008) identified factors that African American male community college students consider in their decision to persist in completing their educations. These factors included the use of time on campus and outside of class, faculty interaction, peer interaction, campus involvement, and utilization of institutional resources. Foster also found that African American male students need to be engaged with faculty who accommodate different learning styles. A welcoming college personnel and an open campus environment promote satisfaction among students. This often encourages students who might be wavering in their decision to stay, which in turn boosts retention of underrepresented students.

St. John, Paulsen, and Carter (2005) found that financial assistance had an outsized impact on college choice and persistence for minority students. This study was on the impact of socio-economic status and amount of financial assistance received on college choice and persistence by race. Their study showed that African-American students are more likely to make decisions about persistence and dropping out based on finances—in particular, affordable tuition charges and available grants encouraged them to continue, as opposed to loans or work-study positions.

The persistence of minority students is related in complex ways to sense of belonging and stereotype threats. Beasley and Fischer (2011) used data from the National Longitudinal
Survey of Freshmen, and determined that in STEM majors, minorities (and also women) are subject to stereotype threats that significantly increase their chances of dropping out of those programs. With this in mind, education theorists have stressed (O'Keeffe, 2013) that colleges must work deliberately to establish a sense of belonging among minority students. O'Keeffe (2013) indicated that minority college students are especially vulnerable to feelings "that they don't belong, feel rejected, and [feel unable to] adjust to normal academic challenges associated with college life," and these feelings are directly linked to diminished persistence.

However, retention programs designed to acculturate minority students can improve persistence, especially when the programs are properly structured and focused on building meaningful interpersonal relationships. Brooks, Jones, and Burt (2013) added a mentorship element to an existing retention program at a large university in the southern U.S. They found that African-American male participants in this study stated having stronger relationships with mentors, better university academic acculturation, and improved social integration into the university community. The most noteworthy impact for these significant results is possibly the creation of staff (coordinator's position) to be solely responsible to the retention initiative/effort; whereas in previous years, various staff persons would oversee the program in addition to their existing duties (Brooks, Jones, & Burt, 2013, pp. 217–218).

Brooks et al.'s (2013) results are significant because they reinforce the idea we have begun to encounter again and again: the establishment of meaningful, academic-personal relationships is one crucial component of retention. In the Brooks et al. (2013) study, African American students met with the same mentor, with the same peers, at the same time each week, and this structure allowed social interaction that was predictable and regular. Other persistence programs should keep in mind this important finding: retention services work best when they are based on the building of socially strong learning communities.

Online/distance-learning students. In the last 10 years, the number of postsecondary education distance learning programs, especially those designed for nontraditional students at for-profit colleges, has ballooned, and with this growth, a drop in levels of student retention has become a significant problem. Studies have suggested that "elements of culture, motivation, learning management systems and online pedagogy play a major role in attrition rates in the higher education sector" (Colferai & Gregory, 2015). What follows here is a discussion of online attrition, its causes, and some possible remedies.

By the late 1990s, the online courses at American institutions grew 200%, and by 2002, more than 57% of all students were enrolled in at least one online course (Colferai & Gregory, 2015). These same authors noted that in financial terms, expenditure on online courses will increase from

$166.5 billion in 2015 to $255 billion in 2017. However, attrition from online courses is 10% to 20% higher than attrition from in-person classes. Furthermore, even though online courses offer the options and freedoms desired by many nontraditional students, studies show that those same students have an even higher risk of attrition from distance-courses than traditional students do (Stoessel, Ihme, Barbarino, Fisseler, & Stürmer, 2015).

In search of a reason for the high online attrition rates among nontraditional students, Stoessel etc all. (2015) conducted a study of more than 6,000 current and former students at the *Fernuniversität* in Germany. With over 90,000 students and no physical campus, the school is similar to fully online institutions found in Europe, Canada, and the United States. Stoessel et al. examined three distinct populations: male and female students, younger and older students, and migrant/non-migrant students. For each group, the authors correlated two characteristics with the probability of attrition: personal development and career development. Professional development was present in student respondents who were interested in such things as "opening new career prospects" or "achieving higher income levels" (Stoessel et al., 2015), while students with high personal development reported interest in things like "gaining new perspectives and experiences" or "gaining new knowledge and insights." The groups found to be most at risk were female students with low career development, younger students with low personal development, and migrant students with high personal development.

These results are consistent with what we have learned above from Tinto and Bourdieu: career obligations and work obligations tend to be at odds with each other in nontraditional students, although strong career *aspirations* among nonworking students tend to encourage retention. Likewise, students who identify strongly with a non-native habitus find acculturation to a new academic and national habitus disorienting and alienating enough to affect their persistence. We can also see here that issues relating to personal development and career development are magnified by online courses that can tend to isolate students rather than create strong academic bonds with their professors and fellow students.

Dr. Abel G. Okagbare, Ed.D.

As online distance learning (ODL) is rapidly becoming a world-wide phenomenon, it is worth looking at attrition and retention dynamics in developing countries. Yasmine (2013) conducted a quantitative, data mining study at the Directorate of Distance Education University of North Bengal, West Bengal, India, a rapidly growing online university that serves a largely rural and exceptionally multiethnic/multi-religious population of about 4,500 students. The study examined pre-entry demographic data including "gender, marital and employment status, subject chosen, social status, age and income" (Yasmin, 2013). The highest attrition rates were found among married learners, employed learners, and older learners. Pregnancy, remoteness of residence, and relocation were also strong predictors of attrition from this ODL program. These findings are not inconsistent with what studies in the U.S. have shown, and should be useful to American universities interested in serving rural populations of learners with jobs, spouses, and remote dwellings.

Online distance learning doctoral programs present an interesting case study because they are more likely than undergraduate ODL colleges to cater to an older, nontraditional population of students who have chosen to "go back" to get their PhDs in spite of their career and family obligations. Accordingly, Terrell, Snyder, and Dringus (2012) conducted a quantitative analysis of 17 ODL doctoral students at risk of attrition. "Connectivity" emerged as the central theme of their study, just as it will for us in Parts 2 and 3 (below). The formation of meaningful interpersonal relationships is without question a central key to persistence. Terrell et al. focused on communication between students, and also between students and faculty, with the aim of investigating the relationship between interpersonal communication and attrition. Students in this program expressed that communicative relationships, while not impossible in theory to create, were nonetheless uncommon. Dissertation advisors, also, were (even when well-liked) uncommunicative in the sense that their written feedback was not often delivered in a timely, dialogical way (Terrell, Snyder, & Dringus, 2012). As communication begins to emerge for us here as a crucial component of educational success, it will be interesting to have a look at that group that has grown up with and most dramatically transformed the way we bond, communicate, and transmit information: Millennials.

Millennial students. Educational theorists have long understood that the transition to college life is difficult because it requires a change of habitus, an adoption of new norms, and the relinquishing of long-held others—a process Tinto called "transformation" (Corwin & Cintrón, 2011, p. 26). At the same time, successful acculturation is accelerated by the formation of meaningful relationships within the college community. Especially important are close friendships, social networks, and peer-to-peer interactions (Corwin & Cintrón, 2011, p. 28). In the absence of these things, the risk of attrition increases.

Interestingly, however, is the fact the Millennials are the first generation to enter college already embedded in a network of virtual relationships and social media connections. Given this, we might ask: How do virtual social networks relate to the college acculturation process? Even before the advent of Facebook and Twitter, the complex social networks found in universities were fully understood by theorists. For example, as late as 2011, Corwin and Cintrón brought a phenomenological method to bear on the question of social networks by making brick-and-mortar observations in a university cafeteria and food court. The researchers found that students tended to sit closest to their old friends, slightly farther away from their new friends, somewhat far from acquaintances, and at a distance from strangers. But as students persisted in college and matured, acquaintances and strangers began to take on meaningful roles for these first-year learners. This simple model of concentric social circles is a starting point for understanding the college acculturation process on the ground as opposed to in virtual space.

Today, however, social media networks have begun to be studied as they relate to the first-year acculturation process. Yang and Brown (2015) studied Facebook use among college freshmen at a large Midwestern university and assessed its role in first-year social adjustment. Their results, however, were inconclusive, suggesting that Facebook was a useful adjustment tool only if students had certain positive attitudes about the usefulness of various Facebook functions, and if they in fact used those functions. The complex picture that emerges from this study suggests that more research and more data will be needed before any strong conclusions can be drawn about social media and college acculturation.

However, educational theorists have had some success in characterizing the Millennial student. Turner and Thompson (2014) noted that Millennials have "socialization characteristics [that] challenge the traditional programs, services, and instructional strategies offered by many colleges" (p. 94). Scholars like Lowery (2004) have claimed that Millennials have exaggerated self-confidence that hinders their critical thinking skills, while other studies cited by Yang and Brown (2014) have characterized Millennials as sheltered, team-players, conventional, confident, achievers, special, and pressured (p. 94).

As for the effects of personal technology and social media, some scholars have associated them with principally negative educational outcomes. Elam, Stratton, and Gleason (2007) have claimed that "An over exposure and dependence on communication mechanisms have decreased the ability of millennial students to resolve conflict, critically think, and develop face to face communication techniques" (Elam, Stratton, & Gleason, 2007). The authors go on to note that some researchers also fear that Millennial students, being over-reliant on communications technology, will have stunted interpersonal (face-to-face) skills. Others have expressed similar concerns that the ease with which Millennial students routinely engage in multitasking behaviors, enabled in part through the use of technology, has shortened their collective attention span. Finally, having completed primary and secondary curricula that may unintentionally encourage rote learning, these students may lack the skills necessary to be critical thinkers or demonstrate introspection and self-reflection (Elam et al., 2007).

That said, it would be a mistake to regard Millennials learners as a new thing under the sun. No matter how complex and ambiguous their generation or its social groups may or may not be, Turner and Thompson (2014) concluded their interviews with dropout freshmen by noting that four very familiar, time-tested themes surfaced when the dropouts were asked about the obstacles and the empowerments they had encountered during their freshman year. The themes were "organized in order by priority: freshmen-focused activities, developing effective study skills, instructor-student relationship, and academic advisements-support" (Turner & Thompson, 2014, p. 103). It is of particular interest that three of these four themes are centered upon meaningful social relationships. This is a theme we will explore further as we investigate the qualities of institutions that are more able, and less able, to retain their students through graduation.

Part Two

Institutional Characteristics: Which Schools Keep Students?

Having examined the qualities of students who are more and less successful in persisting in college, we are in a position now to examine the types of schools in which students tend to persist, and in which, in general, they are at a higher risk of dropping out. We will also have a look at some contemporary efforts by universities to harness big data analytics to track student performance, make timely interventions in the cases of struggling students, and generally to stem attrition through the analysis of information.

Understandably, student attrition is a significant concern among educational leaders because of the negative effects it can have not only on the careers of dropouts, but also on the image of a school (Ackerman et al., 2009). Naturally, both individual and institutional factors have been found to affect student persistence and attrition (Sontam & Gabriel, 2012; Weiss, Carolan, & Baker-Smith, 2010). However, most studies on student attrition focus on the individual characteristics of students we examined above: race, age, socio-economic background, gender, and so on (Bowden & Wood, 2011; Dwyer et al., 2013).

Past research on the institutional factors that affect student attrition in higher education is not as extensive as the literature that focuses on student characteristics, but several institutional factors have been identified as contributing to student attrition (DesJardins & McCall, 2010; Sparks & Nuñez, 2014). To address student attrition, leaders of educational institutions should also focus on institutional factors that may reduce student attrition and improve retention (Nichols, 2010). Based on a review of the extant literature, the following institutional factors can be seen to play roles in the attrition of college students: (a) size of institution, (b) access to student services, (c) availability of financial aid, (d) geographic location, (e) ratio of full- to part-time faculty, (f) a college's for-profit status, and (g) a college's use of big data analytics to track student performance and attrition risk (Arendt, 2013; Barrow, Brock, & Rouse, 2013; Yu, 2014).

Size of Institution

The size of an institution, which can be measured in terms of its ratio of students to the number of educators in the faculty, can have a significant influence on student retention (Lin, Yu, & Chen, 2012). Generally speaking, the overall level of engagement of students tends to increase as the size of a school increases (Weiss et al., 2010). In terms of student retention, Lin, Yu, and Chen (2012) found that students from larger schools tend to have higher retention when compared to students from smaller schools. Similarly, Yu (2014) found that the size of an educational institution can influence the program completion of college students. While the relationship between institution size and attrition is significant, so is class size, and the findings from past studies generally indicated that large classes tend to pose challenges for both instructors and students (Mulryan-Kyne, 2010), while at the same time, large classes are most often found at large universities, all things being equal.

Accessibility of Student Services

Access to student services is important in postsecondary education to help students cope with various challenges experienced in college (Bettinger, Boatman, & Long, 2013; Gansemer-Topf, Zhang, Beatty, & Paja, 2014). Accordingly, the availability or absence of student services is an institutional factor that can influence the attrition of college students (Lin et al., 2012). However, not all student services are equal when it comes to promoting persistence and, in short, the most successful student services are those that build substantial, communicative, lasting relationships between students, as well as between students and faculty. These relationships promote the accrual of the kind of academic social capital that we examined above in our discussion of Bourdieu. In any case, institutional expenditure on student services has been found to be *negatively* correlated with student attrition in higher education, which means that higher expenditure on student services is associated with lower rates of student attrition (Chen, 2012). The range of student services that educational institution leaders can provide may include financial aid such as loans, mentoring, and academic support services (Leeds et al., 2013).

Several researchers have found evidence of the effectiveness of student services for improving student retention and preventing attrition (Hagel, Horn, Owen, & Currie, 2012; Leeds et al., 2013; Swecker, Fifolt, & Searby, 2013). For instance, remediation courses are helpful to students who are not performing well academically, especially those students who had poor academic achievement in high school (Bettinger et al., 2013), and so the availability of curricular programs such as remediation courses can positively influence the retention of college students (Lin et al., 2012). However, only students who need remediation should be put in these courses, given the limited financial resources of many postsecondary institutions (Bettinger et al., 2013), and, also, given the limited financial resources of those students who must pay for remedial courses before advancing to non-remedial, intro-level, and/or mandatory classes.

Other student services that have been found to have some influence on student persistence and attrition are university libraries, campus jobs and housing, academic advising, and mentoring programs (Drake, 2011; Hagel et al., 2012). For example, the availability of campus jobs and on-campus residence can influence retention positively (Lin et al., 2012). And, perhaps surprisingly, the availability and quality of university libraries can also contribute to the retention of students (Hagel et al., 2012), and this is a timely finding at a moment when many universities are choosing to scale back library budgets and funnel the savings to non-academic programs like collegiate athletics.

Academic advising is another important student service that can influence student retention and persistence (Drake, 2011). Empirical evidence showed that as the number of academic advising sessions between teachers and students increases, the likelihood for retention of students also increases (Swecker et al., 2013). Mentoring programs have also been found to be effective in increasing the academic achievement and graduation rate of disadvantaged college students enrolled in undergraduate STEM courses (Wilson et al., 2012).

When compared with other retention strategies such as the promotion of student engagement and student learning communities, the availability of student services emerges as the most effective retention strategy (Leeds et al., 2013). However, contrary to the findings of Leeds et al. (2013) and Lin et al. (2012), there is some evidence that students appreciate the availability of student services, but these services do not influence persistence of students enrolled in distance education (Nichols, 2010). This finding is striking at a moment when more and more courses, especially at for-profit universities, are being offered online or as in-person/online hybrids. Anecdotal reports and in-house studies within a writing program at a large, public university in the Northeast have shown that students with low conscientiousness, poor study habits, and a history of past failures fare poorly in, and drop out of, online courses at a higher rate when compared to higher-achieving students.

In sum, the absence of student services is noticeable to students even though some studies indicate that not all student services positively affect persistence (Nichols, 2010). And, finally, some studies indicate that student affairs remain an important factor that can influence the attrition of college students (Gansemer-Topf et al., 2014).

Availability of Financial Aid

The pursuit of higher education is a significant financial cost for many college students (Barrow et al., 2013). Government leaders recognize the importance of postsecondary education, which is why there are increased efforts to make financial aid available to college students (Barrow et al., 2013). Financial aid can alter how students from low-income families spend their time, which can affect attrition (Goldrick-Rab, Harris, & Benson, 2011). However, based on past studies, the effects of financial aid in increasing persistence and reducing student attrition have not been shown to be definitive (Arendt, 2013; DesJardins & McCall, 2010). A number of studies have argued that receiving any kind of financial aid can reduce the rate of student attrition (Chen & DesJardins, 2010; Melguizo, Torres, & Jaime, 2011), while other studies have indicated that financial aid can reduce student attrition but not the completion of degree programs (Arendt, 2013). On the basis of these conflicting findings, it would seem that further research on the relationship of financial aid to persistence is warranted.

There is some empirical evidence that the type of financial aid available to college students can influence attrition and the likelihood of program completion (DesJardins & McCall, 2010; Melguizo et al., 2011). Specifically, loans and grants can reduce the attrition rate of college students, especially during the first year of college (Melguizo et al., 2011). Interestingly, the positive effects of financial aid tend to be highest during the first year of college (Wang et al., 2013). However, even though the process of acquiring financial aid, such as loans from Free Application for Federal Student Aid (FAFSA), has recently been simplified and streamlined, in the past it was a more complex process that sometimes discouraged students from pursuing financial assistance, leading Barrow et al. (2013) to recommend the simplification of the financial aid application process.

Geographic Location

As we saw above in our look at a distance-education program in India, the geographical location of schools, and of their students, can affect attrition among some student populations, while at the same time, the relationship of a school's location to its attrition statistics is not yet entirely clear (Byun, Irvin, & Meece, 2012; Sparks & Nuñez, 2014; Yu, 2014). Studies indicate that there is no significant difference in the persistence of students from rural, suburban, and urban institutions (Sparks & Nuñez, 2014). Consistent with this lack of difference between rural and non-rural schools, Byun et al. (2012) found that both students from rural and urban schools who are not enrolled in four year programs have similar persistence rates.

At the same time, and contrary to the findings of other authors (i.e., Sparks & Nuñez, 2014, Byun et al., 2012), Yu (2014) found that the geographical location of educational institutions can influence program completion of students. Specifically, Byun et al. found that the rate of college completion of students from rural colleges tend to be different from completion rates at non-rural colleges. There is also an indication that the effectiveness of institutional policies may be affected by the type of geographic location where these policies are being implemented (Groen, 2011).

Ratio of Full-Time to Part-Time Faculty

Part-time or adjunct faculty instructors continue to be hired at higher and higher rates in postsecondary education (Jacoby, 2006). This trend is well-documented and important, given that the percentage of part-time students and faculty in universities can also influence student persistence and attrition, with past studies generally indicating that schools' heavy reliance on part-time faculty does not produce positive student outcomes (Jenicke, Holmes, & Pisani, 2013; Moosai, Walker, & Floyd, 2011). Simply put, numerous studies suggest that, as the use of part-time faculty increases, the rate of attrition among first year students also increases (Jenicke et al., 2013). Similarly, a school's heavy reliance on part-time faculty is negatively correlated with the graduation rate of students (Jacoby, 2006; Moosai et al., 2011). Using three different measures of program completion, Jacoby (2006) found that when the ratio of part-time faculty increases, the rate of graduation also decreases. Nevertheless, the issue is likely more complex than Jacoby has suggested. For example, the results of a study conducted by Yu (2014) contradicted the negative correlation found by Jacoby (2006) and Moosai et al. (2011) between part-time faculty and persistence of students. Instead, Yu (2014) found that part-time faculty does not affect the persistence and program completion of students. Nonetheless, a high level of exposure of first year students to part-time faculty negatively affects the student attrition when those students move to their second year (Jaeger & Egan, 2011). However, given the conflicting findings about the relationship between part-time faculty and student retention in higher education (Jenicke et al., 2013; Moosai et al., 2011; Yu, 2014), we can conclude that more research on this topic is needed.

Student Retention Programs

In the past, most colleges and universities relied on a number of different approaches for helping students in their quests to decide on their majors and pursue their careers. These approaches have had varying levels of success, and have tended not to be helpful when they were not well-integrated with the rest of the collegiate experience. Some retention programs have aimed to help students in determining their majors and their careers, sometimes by means of job shadowing programs, which normally had a low turnout of participation. Other retention programs have focused on internship assistance; freshman career development seminars with inconsistent support from faculty members; career and employment services, which were normally on a volunteer rather than a required basis; career fairs that were attended by select groups of students rather than most or all students; and other special events (McCarthy & McCarthy, 2006). Because the retention problem has become more important due to increased competition among institutions, more schools are beginning to offer actual college career courses (or life planning courses) that are mandatory, graded, and paid for by the students themselves. Such required courses are proving to be effective tools in helping students determine their personal interests, majors, and intended careers (Austin, 2011). These retention strategies—namely job shadowing programs, internship assistance, and career development seminars—can also increase commitment to a school, as Tinto has argued (Austin, 2011).

Certain common problems should be addressed by retention programs if they are to be successful. For example, during a student's first year, factors such as the difficulty of courses, as well as possible mismatches between student and institutional expectations, can come to play in making students drop out of college (Veenstra, 2009). Successful retention programs should seek to identify such mismatches and promote dialogue with students about them. Some attrition problems have roots in student demographics, and so retention programs could also address improving these issues. For example, the level of student-faculty engagement can significantly affect the level of persistence among Latino students (Cejda & Hoover, 2010). However, there are limited studies showing what retention-program strategies should be employed to improve the levels of faculty-student engagement. Teachers' knowledge, appreciation and sensitivity to Hispanic cultures, and teachers' understanding that there are different learning styles among Latino students, can all lead to improved student-faculty engagement and improve college persistence (Cejda & Hoover, 2010).

One model of a successful retention program might be one in which institution administrators, coordinators, advisors, and support personnel collaborate to create an advising system that is advantageous for the school and for its students (Morgan, 2013). When all four of these types of university employees work together to form an effective advising method, they can form a cooperative network that the college can benefit from. This collaboration among diverse employees has been shown by some studies to be capable of creating a dynamic advising system that can improve not only student achievement, but also the rate of student retention (Morgan, 2013).

Commitment to the process of academic advising can also have an important role to play in the success of student retention programs (Heisserer & Parette, 2002). One productive way to encourage students to seek advising support is to develop programs that relate to students' personal needs. The advisor can first help students explore majors and careers and then, once a decision is made, select appropriate courses and arrange schedules. Working in collaboration, the advisors and students can analyze options, gather information, and make decisions together. Collaboration between the advisors and students will increase student involvement in the institution and encourage enrollment until graduation (Morgan, 2013).

Collaboration among the different leaders, educators, and personnel within a college or university can be an important component of its success (Morgan, 2013). A study by Ginsberg and Wlodkowski (2009) claimed that as long as there are school personnel that are ready to support the students, the students will become motivated to learn. Hence, faculty should work to ensure that students' experiences in school are engaging and relevant, and faculty should recognize that not all students have the same experiences and come from the same place; they will all have varying histories and worldviews. Accordingly, administrators, coordinators, and advisors, as well as support staff, can all work together to form a dynamic support system to address the needs of students (Morgan, 2013).

For example, several "persistence programs" have been developed specifically to address retention (Jamelske, 2008; Lillibridge, 2008). These programs are often referred to as First Year Experience (FYE) or Academic Exploration Programs (AEPs). FYE or AEP programs are designed to encourage students to continue their education. While these programs differ from school to school, they all have an element in common, which is their goal of comfortably acculturating and integrating new students into the college or university lifestyle. Researchers have noted that students often find adjusting to college to be an unsettling process. Oftentimes, students get disoriented and feel hesitant, and these feelings hinder students as they attempt to adapt to college life. Accordingly, FYE and AEP programs are established to help in the transition of students from high school to college. Some programs have a specific curriculum to ensure that students are integrated into the college comfortably. Certain courses are identified at the beginning that will allow flexibility to accommodate the development of varying interests in each student. These programs assist students in identifying the academic interests, skill sets, and career options that are in line with their personal goals.

AEP programs provide students with the support they need, the guidance, and the tools to determine the academic direction they want to take. Personal attention is also given to students in a manner that is similar to what they were accustomed to in their earlier education. Weekly seminar classes, individualized academic advising, academic curriculum exhibits hosted by faculty members, and job shadowing opportunities are some of the activities in dynamic programs like AEP.

A specific example of an AEP-like program that has been studied by researchers was one used and developed by the University of Arkansas and called FAST (Freshman Academic Support Tracking). The program consisted of nine hours of classwork in the fall and an additional six hours in the spring. Both of these course programs were supplemented by weekly meetings between students and their mentors (Mangold, Bean, Adams, Schwab, & Lynch, 2002). The authors of the study concluded that the FAST program positively influenced the graduation and retention rates of University of Arkansas students. The authors also concluded that higher and lower grade point averages in high school can be positively and negatively correlated with college dropout rates. Furthermore, and quite interestingly, Mangold et al. (2002) found that students taking lighter course-loads are more likely to drop out as compared to students who take regular course-loads. The authors further investigated the factors that can influence student departure, identifying nine factors: academic advising, administration, social opportunities, enrollment management, faculty development, faculty reward system, student orientation, residential life, and student affairs programming.

Yet another strategy to address low retention rate is mentoring. This practice has been used by colleges and universities to improve the experience of students. The integration of mentoring programs into the collegiate environment is a way for colleges and universities to address student retention, increase diversity in faculty and students, and to increase career networking opportunities (Campbell & Campbell, 1997). Some researchers have showed that mentoring programs have been successful in their goal of supporting students by providing college experiences such as perceived academic supportiveness and social connection. Mentoring has also been identified as a successful strategy with underrepresented populations like African American students (Flowers, 2006; Guiffrida, 2005; Redman Mingo, 2010).

In sum, well-crafted persistence programs can play an important role in reducing student attrition rates and improving student retention (Walters & McCay, 2005). Addressing student attrition rates and retention rates should be part of the school's strategic plan, and the responsibility for that strategic planning should fall to a school's top administrators: Mitchel (2003), for example, has indicated that resource allocation to influence retention should be a core responsibility of a college's or university's administration. Moreover, school plans to improve retention rates will necessitate institutional changes as well, and hence require systematic implementation.

Nevertheless, the complete retention of all students is not possible because of the existence of various factors that may not always be controllable, which led Sibson, Gregory, and Kurisky (2014) to conclude that retention programs should focus on those students who can be retained. There are also a small number of scholars (Sykes, 1996) who do not believe that retention programs are effective. Sykes (1996) further indicated that the "concept of a learning community in which all members share the same vision and responsibility for learning and personal growth" (p. 99) is a notably effective way to retain students.

Past research, however, indicates that the experience of students from traditional not-for profit universities and for-profit universities can be different (Rovai & Downey, 2010; Sibson, Gregory, & Kurisky, 2014). In the next section, the retention of students enrolled in for-profit universities will be discussed to provide an overview of what researchers have found to be the specific retention advantages and challenges facing institutions of this increasingly prevalent type.

Retention of Students in For-Profit Universities

Retention programs are often geared towards students enrolled in traditional and not for-profit universities and colleges (Sibson et al., 2014), but student retention is one of the key factors that can determine the success of for-profit universities, underscoring the importance of exploring different strategies to minimize attrition and improve persistence for program completion (Carroll, Ng, & Birch, 2013; Sibson et al., 2014). And, crucially, effective retention programs can maximize the limited resources of educational institutions (Carroll et al., 2013). The retention of students in for-profit universities poses significant and unique challenges compared to student retention in traditional non-profit universities because of the differences between the students enrolled in these very different types of educational institutions (Sibson et al., 2014).

Many college students who are enrolled in for-profit universities are older adults who have obligations to fulfill to their families, have limited time to devote to their studies, and often have limited financial resources as well (Sibson et al., 2014; Yu & Ertl, 2014). Moreover, many students in for-profit universities, particularly students enrolled in online education, are only exploring their options in the first few semesters (Boston et al., 2011). The implication here is that the exploratory nature of the motivation of students may contribute to the high attrition rate of students enrolled in for-profit universities and colleges (Boston et al., 2011).

In the academic year of 2008–2009 in for-profit universities, as many as one million students dropped out with massive debts and without diplomas (Lansing & Olsen, 2011), but leaders in for-profit higher education have developed programs to support student retention (Austin, 2011; Jaeger & Eagan, 2011). Previous researchers have also noted that policymakers have developed programs and initiatives that intend to improve student retention (Jaeger & Eagan, 2011; Keller, 2009). Given the high attrition rate of students in for-profit universities, and especially in distance learning environments, there is pressure from educational leaders to provide support that can reduce student attrition (Street, 2010). But despite showing some success in reducing student retention, programs designed to help retain students have been reduced as a result of lack of state support (Keller, 2009). Research has shown that retention efforts should focus on college students who are only exploring their options in the first few courses that they take, given the high likelihood of attrition when these students' expectations are not met (Boston et al., 2011). The findings of Boston et al. (2011) are consistent with the findings of Willcoxson, Cotter, and Joy

(2011), who found that student attrition tends to be at the highest during the first year of college, which underscores the importance of addressing the needs of first year college students in order to increase retention.

With regard to attrition and retention, the behaviors of students enrolled in for-profit universities, and especially those that that are fully online institutions, are affected by influences that can be categorized as follows: (a) course factors, (b) environmental factors, and (c) person factors (Street, 2010). Course factors include the relevance and design of courses; environmental factors include family support, organizational support, and technical support; and person factors include self-efficacy, self-determination, autonomy, and time management skills (Street, 2010). Consistent with the model generated by Smart (2010), several strategies have been proposed to improve the retention of students in for-profit universities and colleges (Needham, Nurse, Parker, Scantlebury, & Dick, 2013), and these retention strategies targeted the three factors mentioned above (Boston et al., 2011; Hagel et al., 2012; Needham et al., 2013).

One of the important contributors to persistence that is lacking in many for-profit universities and colleges, and especially those offering only or primarily distance education, is the kind of social activity that is typical in traditional and not for-profit universities. Student engagement is an important component of the academic experience of college students (Gooden & Martin, 2014). And, as we saw in Part 1 above, academic social capital, as well as meaningfully communicative relationships between students and faculty, are crucial to the minimization of attrition. The interaction of students with faculty members and other students is a typical part of the experience of many college students, but such interaction may not be an option available in many for-profit universities and colleges. Educational leaders of for-profit universities should consider efforts that increase the social activity of students (Boston et al., 2011).

As noted above, student services such as university libraries can improve the persistence of students (Hagel et al., 2012), leading Needham et al. (2013) to question if online libraries can influence retention of students enrolled in distance learning. Utilizing technology in ways that can support students may minimize the challenges in the college experience (Barrow et al., 2013). Some of the examples in which technology can help students include the availability of online registration and the use of online learning communities (Barrow et al., 2013).

However, attrition from for-profit universities, although clearly a significant problem for both the schools and their students, also provides a unique opportunity for us to gain comparative insight into how attrition and retention work in a general sense. This is true precisely because the for-profit school differs in such clear ways from its traditional counterparts. For this reason, in Part 3 of this book, we will turn to an in-depth case study of one for-profit university with persistence rates that varied markedly among 10 of its campuses. We will learn, through an analysis of the words of faculty members and administrators themselves, useful lessons that can be applied in diverse higher education institutions interested in improving student retention.

Big Data Analytics as a Retention Strategy

Perhaps not surprisingly, in an age dominated by the flow of large quantities of information, universities have begun to recognize the power of data analytics to predict student success and to make adjustments as needed. In fact, in just the past five years, *learning analytics* (LA) and *educational data mining* (EDM) have emerged as powerful tools with the potential to predict students' educational outcomes. Learning analytics, which combines tools deployed in business intelligence systems and web analytics, among other fields, was defined at the First International Conference on Learning Analytics and Knowledge (LAK), as "the measurement, collection, analysis and reporting of data about learners and their contexts, for purposes of understanding and optimizing learning and environments in which it occurs" (Papamitsiou & Economides, 2014). Likewise, EDM is "concerned with 'developing, researching, and applying computerized methods to detect patterns in large collections of educational data that would otherwise be hard or impossible to analyze due to the enormous volume of data within which they exist" (Romero & Ventura, 2013, p. 12, as cited in Papamitsiou & Economides, 2014).

At the present time, LA and EDM are just emerging from the research and development phase, but a growing number of commercial LA suites and products, like Blackboard Analytics and Mulce, are already available to institutions of higher learning, and experts expect that most colleges and universities will have begun to implement some form of LA within 1–2 years (Reyes, 2015). In this last section of Part 2, we will look at some approaches to LA that have been studied within the past several years.

Universities are well suited to data mining because they are above all *complex* systems in which many variables and influences are in play. Indeed, some researchers have taken the technical term "complexity" from physics and situated it in an educational context. In physics, and in other scientific disciplines that employ the complexity thinking, "complex" phenomena are large systems in which orderly patterns and structures seem to emerge spontaneously as an apparently unintended result of the sometimes chaotic interactions of the smaller, individual components of these systems. Classic examples of such complexity are the forms and patterns that emerge in the seemingly coordinated motions of schools of fish and flocks of birds. Such patterns manifest as webs consisting of interconnected factors and influences that are unevenly distributed. Within this web-like network, these factors manifest as concentrated in some places and diffused in others, but always without expressing a top-down hierarchy.

The application of complexity thinking to the problem of university attrition was proposed in 2014 by Forsman, Linder, Moll, Fraser, and Andersson, who examined the persistence behavior of engineering and physics students at a Swedish university by presenting the students with a lengthy questionnaire. The survey was composed of 29 questions concerning a range of things; it sought demographic, financial, and academic information, as well as information pertaining to students' subjective feelings about their experiences in courses and in school generally. This last type of question asked students if they agreed or disagreed with statements such as "I have developed a good relationship with my teachers in the courses I have studied" or "First year physics courses have been inspiring" (Forsman et al., 2014, p. 76). From the students' answers, the authors used a technique called multidimensional scaling analysis to create a web-like visualization of the interconnectedness of retention with other "nodes" of the students' educational data, where a factor such as "friends' opinions of institutional quality" might interconnect and form a node with "feeling of belonging of the university" (Forsman et al., 2014). Although this particular study was not predictive, it did demonstrate that universities are classically complex, and that the tools used by cosmologists and geneticists can be used, too, by educators to model attrition in relation to a dizzying network of interconnected factors.

Other educational researchers have begun to use LA and EDM in alternate ways to arrive at similarly useful conclusions. As data processing methods have been refined, the predictive accuracy of EDM programs has increased. For example, researchers in Taiwan used institutional review (IR) data to create an EDM analysis system that predicted dropouts from a Taiwanese university with nearly an 85% level of accuracy (Lin, 2015). Systems this accurate hold out the possibility that universities might create early warning systems (EWS) for students at risk of attrition (Lin, 2015).

In fact, researchers have begun to approach the study of EDM and LA from many angles. Some studies from the previous decade began by bringing machine learning technologies to bear on aggregated student identity information, while other studies experimented with a range of student-classification algorithms to see which could best predict attrition based on student data taken from the first year of enrollment (Papamitsiou & Economides, 2014). In the present decade, some researchers have used EDM to link attrition to data revealing students' levels of engagement with synchronous online activities. Even neural network techniques are being introduced to LA, and all of these examples serve to show that a wide range of computational strategies and technologies hold out the promise that early warning systems based on EDM are or will soon be within the reach of those educational institutions with the resources to afford and implement them.

LA and EDM strategies are also being developed with a particularly at-risk population in mind: part-time students in distance learning programs, where completion rates hover around the 50% mark (Calvert, 2014). Predictive analytics, a branch of computer science that focuses on ascertaining future events, has been shown to be an especially promising tool for studying the part-time distance learner. In 2014, Carol Elaine Calvert conducted a study at the Open University UK (OUUK) using a classic, statistical, "big data" approach that cross-referenced two main bodies of data: general student records, and data showing the path of students through individual educational milestones measured mostly in terms of study-module completions and periodic payment of fees. The amount of data in this instance was truly massive, and was comprised of hundreds of data points per student, hundreds of thousands of students, and five years' worth of records. The student records were comprehensive and included socio-demographic data, information on students' goals and reasons for attending the university, the students' paths of study, and successes or failures within the "modules" they completed. The researcher was able to create a predictive model of student success with an accuracy level that increased along with the students' progress from milestone to milestone, and which in some cases approached 95% accuracy (Calvert, 2014, p. 170). The methods used in this study are particularly relevant to universities that wish to focus on curriculum development, because predictive analytics modeling can help universities identify way-stations and academic milestones at which students of certain types tend to face high risks of failure or attrition.

Given the complexity of the data that LA systems like this one can yield, it is essential that educators and college administrators have access to information in a way that is visually intuitive. Given this, substantial effort is being made to improve the data visualization provided by LA systems (Reyes, 2015), although it is difficult in general to represent the results of big data analysis in a way that is graphically intuitive and/or interactive.

Perhaps more importantly, it is crucial to remember why learning analytics are important in the first place, and the answer has been suggested forcefully by Verbert et al. (2012) who indicated that it is the experience of the learner that is most essential, and this experience is something above and beyond the question of whether or not a given learner persists in his or her studies until graduation. Rather, LA systems should "predict learner performance, suggest learning resources relevant to the learner, increase reflection and awareness, enhance social learning, detect undesirable behaviors, and detect learner affects" (Verbert et al., 2012, as cited in Reyes 2015, p. 78).

What can be lost in the data, however, are the phenomenal, concrete, and verbally expressed feelings and experiences of individual learners and educators, and it is for that reason the we shall turn now in Part Three to a case study with great potential to illuminate the national problem of attrition: the case of a for-profit university and its struggle with problems of student retention, as expressed in the words of the decision makers for whom these problems are a central concern.

Part Three

Best Practices to Keep Students in School: A Case Study

Now that we have established the factors affecting student attrition and retention, it is time to look at these issues on a more practical level, through the voices of decision makers with first-hand experience on what works. In 2014, I completed a qualitative case study on the institutional factors that enhance student retention. I spoke with faculty members and school administrators at 10 campuses of a large for-profit university to find out directly what boosts student retention and encourages persistence. By looking at this university, we can learn more about how to help other institutions of higher education—for-profit and non-profit alike—to improve their retention rates.

The For-Profit Institution Model

A lot of the conversation in the field of higher education has focused on "for-profit" institutions, or colleges and universities that are managed and governed as privately held companies (Deming, Goldin, & Katz, 2013). As the name implies, these institutions tend to emphasize maximizing profits rather than functioning as a public entity or a non-profit organization. They are often distinguished by their flexibility in delivering educational services through distance learning, online education, and/or night and weekend schooling (Sibson et al., 2014; Yu & Ertl, 2014). A lot of the faculty is part-time, and some split their time between education and other industries.

In recent years, the market share of for-profit colleges and universities has exploded: from 1970 to 2009, enrollment in for-profit universities increased from 0.2% to 9.1% (Belfield, 2013; Deming, Goldin, & Katz, 2012). Today, more than 2 million of the 19 million college students in the United States are enrolled in for-profit institutions (Wilson, 2010). Because of these institutions' flexible programs and less rigorous admissions practices, many of these students are adults who may not have qualified for admission to other schools. Additionally, compared to other types of institutions, private for-profit universities have a greater number of minority students (Deming et al., 2012).

However, in recent years, some for-profit colleges and universities have been accused of illegal or unethical practices in their pursuit of greater profits and more efficient educational delivery systems. One company, for example, closed in 2015 after several state and federal lawsuits regarding its job placement statistics and lending practices. Other for-profit institutions have faced increased scrutiny of their recruitment practices, graduation rates, and student-loan default statistics. Perhaps as a result of these investigations and consequent bad publicity, many for-profit schools have seen their enrollments decline severely, particularly in the past three years.

Although scandals have spurred calls to eliminate the for-profit sector, such a drastic measure would be both unwise and unrealistic. For-profit institutions offer access to higher education for many kinds of students—adult learners, working professionals, students with families—that would find it extremely difficult to complete degrees at traditional colleges and universities. Additionally, the privately-held, corporate nature of these institutions' governing bodies allows them maximum flexibility when making operational changes or implementing programs to improve outcomes for their students. As such, as we will see, the for-profit institution can function as a laboratory to test student retention strategies that may also work for other types of institutions, including public and private non-profit colleges and universities.

The Case Study

Participants. In my study, I interviewed administrators and faculty members who were employed at different campuses at a private, for-profit university. Despite being part of the same institution, the university's multiple campuses have very different rates of student retention. The campuses have different demographic profiles, different levels of resources, and different strategies in place to encourage student persistence and maximize student retention. As the campuses operate somewhat independently under the umbrella of a large university, speaking with members across the campuses thus presented a unique opportunity to study potential solutions to the student retention problem in different yet connected environments.

Initially, I contacted 30 educators from the institution about the study; 15 from campuses with high student retention rates, and 15 from campuses facing challenges with student persistence. Of these initial thirty, I narrowed it down to 10 participants, six men and four women. Seven participants were administrators and three were faculty; all were directly involved in student instruction and/or retention, and all served on the Persistence Committee at their campus. Their tenures at the university ranged from six months to seven years, although those who were new to their positions had extensive prior experience in the education sector. I grouped the participants equally by whether they came from "High Persistence Locations" (HPL) or "Low Persistence Locations" (LPL). Table 1 shows the demographic information—gender, age, and time in position—for each of the 10 participants.

Table 1: *Demographic Characteristics of the Participants*

Pseudonym	Gender	Age	Title	Time at University	Time on the Student Persistence Committee
P1-HPL	Females	64	Dean of Academic Affairs	20 years	20 years
P2-LPL	Male	[Past Retirement Age]	Senior Professor	16 years	8 years
P3-HPL	Male	50	Senior Professor	13 years	-
P4-HPL	Male	49	Dean of Academic Affairs	20 years	5 years
P5-LPL	Female	50	Dean of Students' Affairs	5 years	2 years
P6-HPL	Female	Late 40s	Dean of Academic Affairs	6 months	6 months
P7-LPL	Male	-	-	-	-
P8-LPL	Male	42	Area President	7 months	17 years
P9-LPL	Female	40	Associate Professor	2 years	4 months
P10-HPL	Male	67	Dean of Academic Affairs	6 years	[unknown]

Methods. I approached the study as a multiple case study. Rather than examine the institution as one site, I studied each campus as a different yet connected site, which allowed me to determine the different ways that each campus approached and viewed student retention. Interviews provided the bulk of data collected. First, before conducting the interviews with participants, I conducted a field test with a panel of experts in education to make sure that all proposed interview questions were clear and could generate useful and relevant responses. After the field test, to gather the data, I then conducted in-depth, semi-structured face-to-face and/or phone interviews. The interviews generally lasted between 30 and 45 minutes, and took place at various locations convenient to the participants. I recorded all interviews for later transcription and analysis, with the permission of the participants. In the interviews, I asked participants four structured demographic questions (age, gender, length of service with the university, and length of time serving on the Student Persistence Committee), and five semi-structured questions about student retention:

1. What are the institutional factors that contribute to student retention to address the high drop-out rates in private for-profit universities?
2. What do you view as being the most important institutional factors that can contribute to student retention and why?
3. What do you view as being the least important institutional factors that can contribute to student retention and why?
4. What do you perceive as being the most overrated institutional factors contributing to student retention and why?
5. What do you perceive as being the most underrated institutional factors contributing to student retention and why?

In order to strengthen the integrity of the data, I used data triangulation to analyze different sources of information. I utilized member checking extensively, which involves verifying the researcher's conclusions with the participants themselves, to make sure that I correctly interpreted and understood the interview data. Semester-to-semester campus reports provided an additional source of data. These reports, distributed to campus leaders on a regular basis by the university, included attrition rates for the campuses included in the sample. Although these reports were publicly available, I obtained additional consent from the university to use them in the study.

Because the data came largely from interviews, I used a qualitative method for analysis. With qualitative analysis, I could interpret the rich data generated by the interviews. This analysis began immediately after completing the interviews, at which point I reviewed and transcribed the recordings, and identified initial major themes and recurrent elements in the data. I then further examined these recurrent themes by performing content analysis. This analysis produced coherent thematic categories that reflect the perceptions of the interviewees regarding student retention. Specifically, I used the Krippendorff method of content analysis in order to make valid inferences based on context. This further allowed for inductive analysis to describe the participants' understanding of student attrition and persistence. Such analysis makes data the basis of each category rather than using a previous theoretical framework.

More specifically, to conduct this analysis I used NVivo 10, a computer program for qualitative data analysis. This software allowed me to create categories known as "nodes," and to code them into themes and subthemes, which identified how frequently various recurring words and concepts were present in the data in relation to each interview question. Overall, I identified 14 major categories in the data. Of these categories, 10 were most consistent between the interviews:

1. Academic support,
2. Student persistence,
3. New student orientation (NSO) systems,
4. Institutional factors that contribute to student retention,
5. Most important institutional factors influencing student retention,
6. Least important institutional factors influencing student retention,
7. Overrated institutional factors influencing student retention,
8. Underrated institutional factors influencing student retention,
9. Ways to engage students in the institution, and
10. Best practices for student retention.

These thematic categories became the basis for understanding the common themes across all of the different interviews, as I explain below.

Findings from the Thematic Categories
1. Academic support available in private for-profit universities. This category includes two nodes: the implementation of programs to encourage academic persistence and the creation of student performance monitoring

and evaluation systems. One participant, P2-LPL, said that student persistence could be addressed with "mentors or tutors available during office hours." P7-LPL stressed that the campus offered "the best librarian and library in the college . . . it is marketed aggressively for students who are having difficulty in their studies." Similarly, P5-LPL discussed the services available at her campus:

> We have a tutoring, we have an academic support center that's staffed by student workers, student tutors and that's one of the features that we offer and we try to match up students to that. It's a challenge for that specific demographic that you mentioned, first generation college students, because they are frequently reluctant to admit they don't know something or that they need help because they have a perception that they should be knowing and doing.

P2 and P7, both from the LPL group, stressed that they monitor the involvement of faculty in students' academic lives. P2-LPL stated:

> We do our best to try to monitor professors to make sure that they are active in our class websites, that they are constantly in communication via the course website in terms of class discussions, emails back and forth, announcements.

P7-LPL shared that in order for the university to ensure student persistence in school, the administrators would need to address students' academic difficulties:

> We have both students who tutor and faculty members who tutor, who are signed up specifically to tutor, especially in the more complex courses. Then myself, I offer students who are having difficulty the opportunity to work with me one-on-one to see if we can bring them to together with their peers in the classroom during the semester.

Table 2: *Thematic Category 1. Academic Support Available in the Private For-Profit Universities*

Themes	# of Occurrences	% of Occurrences
Programs that ensure students' persistence	2	20%
Creative lecturing	1	10%

2. Student persistence initiatives in for-profit universities. Eight nodes emerged that addressed specific programs to encourage student persistence: (a) implementation and support of extracurricular activities, (b) improvement of the school system overall, (c) offering financial support, (d) faculty engagement, (e) creative lecturing, (f) comprehensive NSO, (g) active communication with students, and (h) active support services. From these eight nodes, active communication with students, academic support services, and faculty involvement seemed to be top priorities for these participants. Table 3 provides a breakdown of these nodes.

Table 3: *Thematic Category 2. Students' Persistence Initiatives in For-Profit Universities*

Themes	# of Occurrences	% of Occurrences
Faculty involvement	3	30%
Active communication with students	3	30%
Academic support services	3	30%
Improvement of the school system	1	10%
Support for extra and co-curricular activities	1	10%
Implementation of financial schemes	1	10%
Comprehensive NSO	1	10%
Creative lecturing	1	10%

As an example of "active communication with students," the LPL group discussed a system of contacting students who appeared to be at risk of dropping out. P2-LPL stated:

> One is contacting students who meet a certain low end requirement by a certain week in each cycle of classes. For example, if they're below a certain attendance level or participation level in terms of turning in activities. They are individually contacted via

phone and email and counseled if they can be contacted. That one, we've had various names of it. It's been on and off for at least eight years. It seems to have an effect, but it doesn't seem to last very long. They come and go.

P7-LPL explained that this system is mandatory for all faculty members. P7-LPL shared: "The faculty is required to make telephone or email contact with a base number of students to follow up with them, all of it focused on either do you have a problem, have you enrolled in the next semester." P7-LPL further explained:

> There's no relationship marketing with the students to build any kind of a one-on-one relationship so that the student genuinely sees that we're interested in them. It's all about "Are you going to enroll? Is anything happening with people that would keep you from continuing here as a student?"

The HPL group took a different approach to maintaining regular communication with students. P10-HPL stressed that faculty members communicate with students to discuss the career services guidance that the campus could offer:

> The program chair for our accounting department keeps an email list of every students that she's had for the last 12 years and she emails job openings out to that list as she gets them from former students who are now employers. It provides a connectivity to those students even if they're not looking for work or not qualified for the jobs that are being sent out. It's a constant reminder to them of what's out there and what's available and it gives them opportunities to connect, not only back to the university, but with each other. It's a very powerful—not just communication tool—but I think persistence tool.

Under the availability of academic support services, three participants stressed the importance of helping students overcome academic difficulties. P5-LPL identified the academic services available on her campus. She described this as a comprehensive service where students could find almost everything necessary to succeed in school:

> I have been fortunate enough to work with a great team here in my location and implemented success drives or I would say, all school house activities that include academics, career services, the registrar's office, student central, coming together meeting at a central location for the purpose of registering students. The students have an opportunity to have all functional teams in one location to assist and support their registration needs and outcomes. At a particular time during the term, we get together and everyone is there and we invite the students to come in, so if there's an academic issue, if there is a registration hold, you've got the decision makers that are sitting in the room to support the advising and the ability for the student to move forward in the process.

The HPL group had a different idea of how to provide academic support services to students. P6-HPL said that they "[reach] out" to students and "offer support mechanisms for them." These mechanisms include "workshops on these same sorts of topics," and "embedded tutoring in classes that have high risk for failure."

3. New student orientation system in the for-profit university. New student orientation (NSO) was not identified as a student persistence initiative by many of the participants. To look into this aspect further, I asked participants directly about NSOs at their institution. Four nodes emerged in response: (a) establishing expectations, (b) multi-departmental support, (c) ensuring that NSO was information-based, and (d) establishing a welcoming environment. Six participants stressed that NSO was conducted on campus to show the collective effort of every department to provide students with quality services. P2-LPL described the involvement of alumni during NSO:

We have alumni that show up. I take them through a series of four questions that we think new students would like to hear. The alumni (recent grads) go through all that with them. They say, "Okay, first of all, there's somebody that's like me here. I've made a friend and here's some people that actually got through it and how all that worked." Then we try to motivate them, give them motivational speeches, this and that.

Similarly, P7-LPL stressed that department representatives should participate in student orientation. P7-LPL stated, "On a typical person [in an NSO session], we try to have representatives from the faculty from each of the departments present and participate."

Conversely, the HPL group stressed that NSOs were conducted to orient students to the campus, in order to show students how to access services and the resources available to resolve issues. P1-HPL stated:

The NSOs continue to evolve. As we identify issues, we tend to make adjustments that need to be made. For example, on our campus, I'm currently heading now a committee on how [to] provide additional support to international students in terms of an additional international student NSO, because we have a real strong belief that our international students have got some additional needs and concerns that are not addressed in a general NSO.

P3-HPL further shared:

We have the NSO usually the Thursday before the start of the session. I'm involved with the IT component of that. There're different speakers. They come in for—it's probably about two or three hours. They get different orientation[s]; the president speaks to them. They get information on the library; how to work with the registrar. The piece I'm most directly involved [in] there is the online component. I go through how to get into their courses, how to log on to their shell, what the courses look like, [and] where to find the threaded discussions and the dropbox.

Four of the participants clarified that NSOs are conducted on campus to provide the students with a welcoming environment. Both members of the HPL and LPL groups believed in the importance of a welcoming environment for student persistence. P2-LPL shared his intention in joining in an NSO activity:

I definitely try to get to know all the students right off the bat and have them do what I call a warm-up exercise to get to know each other. I make sure that they start to know somebody in their major, and that they can start making friends [so] they can at least start making connections with the place.

P8-LPL supported P2-LPL by explaining this idea further:

To me, I think it's of utmost importance in new student orientation to ensure that the exchange of information is engaging; that it is stimulating and dynamic from the student perspective. It's been my experience that when you can deliver that type of an orientation, the information is much more likely to be retained and the students will be less surprised or shocked if they end up violating one of those policies that might result in dismissal or other disciplinary action.

Table 4 shows the system of NSO practiced in the for-profit university.

Table 4: *Thematic Category 3. System of NSO in the For-Profit University*

Themes	# of Occurrences	% of Occurrences
Multi-departmental support	5	50%
Establish welcoming environment	3	30%
Information-based activity	2	20%
Setting-up of expectations	2	20%

4. **Institutional factors that contribute to student retention.** This thematic category emerged from the aggregation of 10 nodes. These factors include: (a) system of data integration, (b) supportive environment, (c) student preparation, (d) student engagement, (e) offerings of quality services, (f) meeting students' needs, (g) fair policies and procedures, (h) establishment of data, (i) career mentoring, and (j) availability of individuals to help students. Two to five participants responded to six of the 10 nodes. Table 5 shows these factors.

Table 5: *Thematic Category 4. Institutional Factors that Contribute to Student Retention*

Themes	# of Occurrences	% of Occurrences
Offerings of quality services	5	50%
Availability of individual who could help students	2	20%
Students engagement	2	20%
Supportive environment	2	20%
Meeting students' needs	2	20%
Fair policies and procedures	2	20%
Career mentoring	1	10%
System of data integration	1	10%
Establishment of data	1	10%
Students' preparation	1	10%

Five of the participants believed that offering quality services to students influences students' decisions to stay in school. According to P6-HPL, private institutions struggle to improve their systems continuously and prove that they are not solely motivated by financial gain. P6-HPL, a participant who had been previously employed at a public university, stressed this difference in how the public perceives for-profit and nonprofit institutions, saying, "My particular university is very rigorous in the sense of maintaining those standards." P6-HPL believed that maintaining quality services benefitted the students by providing academic tutors who would help them master the difficulties in understanding course material. P6-HPL further stated that their students were surprised when they encountered study requirements:

> Students are coming in expecting to attend 4 hours or 3 hours a week in a particular course, not realizing—or not really fully buying into the idea—that there is a whole other segment in a blended course that's going to require several more hours of time. Then, there's the additional study time that would be expected on top of that.

P8-LPL further explained that offering quality academic services could stimulate students' academic interest. P9-LPL also stressed that public institutions must deliver quality academic services to support the financial costs imposed on their students. P9-LPL said that the university is "look[ing] for more ways to be more cost effective." P9-LPL believed that students are looking for institutions that can support their academic needs at a relatively low cost:

> I believe cost is the number one thing for most for-profit institutions and several private institutions. The cost of tuition overall compared to our competitors in this market. Even if people want to come here because they have a better product, they don't always remain because the funding runs out.

P10-HPL further stated that institutions compete for market share and that this competition dictates the quality of services on the campuses. P10-HPL stated:

> The general economic condition of the market is a factor: the general employment/ unemployment condition of the market that the

particular university is in, the level of institutional competition, how many other schools are trying to compete for the students that they may already.

5. Most important institutional factors influencing student retention.

The most important factors identified by participants that influence student retention are understanding students and establishing teacher-student relationships. These factors were even more important than competitive pricing or affordability for students, or the provision of quality services.

More specifically, three participants believed that retention requires understanding the plight of students. P2-LPL stressed the need to view "each student as an individual and understand their individual attributes that will help them or hinder them on their path toward graduation." P2-LPL commented that a large portion of the student population in private, for-profit universities are nontraditional students who have unique needs:

> A lot of our students, they may be the first one in their family attending college regardless of their age. They may not have a big support network outside of here. We need to make sure that we understand that and not take it for granted.

P2-LPL stressed that the risks of students dropping out of the program will remain unaddressed if administrators do not understand student needs. P4-HPL similarly stated: "unless we develop very intimate relationships with our population at all levels, within all departments, we're not going to be successful in retaining any of our students." P5-LPL also explained that a large number of nontraditional students comprise the private, for-profit university's traditional students. P5-LPL said that with the financial challenges students encounter, the institution may need to implement affordable pricing for those who may decide to drop out due to financial difficulties. P5-LPL stated:

You've got students that are working adults, some are unemployed and utilizing their Department of Education funds to supplement their living expenses. As we continue to increase—not increase our rates, but add these incremental, incidental charges, it still has an impact on those students and their ability to work and live.

P3-HPL alternatively indicated the need for educators to access students' data in order to understand their unique needs:

I think that it would have a big impact if we have access to the data. It's something that already exists, and it's something that we could quickly ramp up, I believe, and we can get access to that so we can identify students early and try different interventions.

Table 6 shows the most important institutional factors influencing student retention.

Table 6: Thematic Category 5. Most Important Institutional Factors Influencing Student Retention

Themes	# of Occurrences	% of Occurrences
Establishment of student-teacher relationship	3	30%
Understanding students	3	30%
Setting of competitive financial scheme	2	20%
Setting-up of expectations	1	10%

6. Least important institutional factors influencing student retention. This category is the combination of three nodes: (a) prioritizing process over outcome, (b) meeting students' needs, and (c) functional facilities. Six of the participants believed that while their institutions had implemented programs that addressed student attrition, the majority of those programs focused on implementation rather than outcomes. For example, P3-HPL shared that their campus tracks emails sent to communicate with students:

> The process is very cumbersome. . . . [It] actually takes more time than e-mail or phone call because it's kind of convoluted. It seems to me that our team president, on a town hall meeting they had 2 weeks ago, talked about focusing on the process rather than the outcomes. I think sometimes we get caught more in the process than the outcomes.

P4-HPL further described this circumstance in relation to the grading system, stating that grades have become the basis for denying admission into college:

> I think sometimes we get too caught up in grades. I know we have to report grades, Abel, because that's part of what we do and that's part of what our regulations require and the accrediting bodies require. It's almost like, to me, just looking at grades, looking at—or I shouldn't just say not only grades—metrics after the fact. If a student gets bad grades, after the fact that we say he probably or she probably doesn't belong in college. If we could develop those relationships [with students] earlier on, they may never make it to getting a bad grade. Don't let the metrics drive what you do. Let the metrics be an outcome of what you do upfront in developing relationships.

P6-HPL added that her institution emphasized meeting campus procedure rather than proactively addressing the possible issues that students may encounter: "We put a tremendous amount of energy around registration. Even on some campuses, going into classrooms, which students get pretty frustrated with I think those kind of efforts are least effective." P8-LPL also shared that there was "too much emphasis placed on nonessential institutional qualities." P9-LPL claimed that the volumes of required calls made by faculty/administrators to students at risk of dropping out did not influence the students' decision to remain in school.

P10-HPL provided additional insight that related to how the institution prioritizes the process over the outcome. He said that the institution implemented standardized learning materials to ensure the standard quality of the learning content:

> Well, I don't have any input into what I teach because this whole thing is developed in Chicago and they're given to me to teach. Making a point that because we have a practitioner-based curriculum, it doesn't really have any impact on whether the student is going to stay or not.

Table 7: *Thematic Category 6. The Least Important Institutional Factors Influencing Retention*

Themes	# of Occurrences	% of Occurrences
Prioritizes process than outcomes	6	60%
Functional facilities	4	40%
Meeting the students' needs	1	10%

7. Overrated institutional factors influencing student retention. Category 7 is the aggregation of seven nodes: (a) marketing strategies, (b) active communication, (c) standardized curriculum, (d) students' satisfaction, (e) admission on the basis of financial capacity, (f) availability of financial aid, and (g) implementation of a freshman program. Two of the participants believed that marketing concepts were among the most overrated factors affecting retention. Only participants from the LPL group mentioned this factor. P2-LPL claimed that "for a for-profit . . . they had an excellent image and they've recently gone under. That shows obviously that those things [i.e., image] do not guarantee success." P9-LPL also shared that while new advertisements were beautiful "and they show a nice level of diversity, they don't show a whole lot of people in classrooms with books."

The second factor that participants thought of as overrated was establishing regular communication with students at risk of dropping out. This theme was mentioned several times by four participants in the study.

However, only two from the LPL group perceived this as an overrated factor of retention. P8-LPL, for example, stated:

> I think if an institution is at the point where they are constantly trying to badger, email and call and harass the student back into class, they are probably at a point that they've missed something. I think at that point, they're in a reactionary stage as opposed to being proactive and developing those relationships. I would concur with that.

Table 8 shows also shows other retention factors less frequently mentioned.

Table 8: Thematic Category 7. Perceived Overrated Institutional Factors Influencing Students' Retention

Themes	# of Occurrences	% of Occurrences
Marketing strategies	2	20%
Active communication	2	20%
Standardized curriculum	1	10%
Students' satisfaction	1	10%
Admission on the basis of financial capacity	1	10%
Availability of financial aid	1	10%
Freshmen program	1	10%

8. Underrated institutional factors influencing student retention. This thematic category is the aggregation of: (a) establishment of student-teacher relationships, (b) faculty empowerment, (c) skill-based instruction, (d) understanding the unique needs of students, (e) student accountability, (f) job placement after college, (g) appreciation of regional differences, (h) campus employment, and (g) access to student information. Six participants believed that an increase in faculty communication with at-risk students had failed to convince those students to remain in school. P4-HPL claimed that this was mainly the result of an absence of personal relationships between faculty and students. He noted that many faculty members established communication with students because they were required to do so and not necessarily because they were committed to understanding the situation of the students personally. P4-HPL stated:

I think going back with some of the faculty members that I had over the years, it was always more of a—it seemed like more of a dictatorship where they told me what I had to do and they told me the information that I needed to do it with. If I didn't do [it], there was a big consequence to it. I think that is probably the factor that could probably hurt you the most. You can't tell [faculty] what to do anymore. You have to ask, listen, then respond.

P8-LPL stated that he could not automatically establish personal relationships with at-risk students. He described how some faculty feel that students should be responsible for establishing relationships with faculty:

Personal relationships can get developed with the student. I think, as academics, we tend to perhaps put ourselves on a pedestal that may be undeserved. We think, "Well, we've earned PhDs or master's degrees. We've paid our dues in the educational system. Therefore, the students should be privileged to be in our presence. I shouldn't have to really get off of my perch and engage with a student. They should climb their way up to me.

Faculty empowerment (i.e., where faculty were given some autonomy) was similarly underrated. This factor was mentioned by six of the participants, however only three perceived this factor as unimportant. The participants mentioned that standardizing the curriculum and monitoring at-risk students affected their productivity as independent educators. A majority of the responses concerning faculty empowerment came from the LPL group. P2-LPL indicated the need for faculty professional development activities:

It's very important to make sure the professors are on their game and they're constantly learning and moving forward and interested and engaged. Maybe put things like doing a little community outreach in their development plans just to make sure that they stay humble and engaged.

Table 9: *Thematic Category 8. Underrated Institutional Factors that Influence Students' Retention*

Themes	# of Occurrences	% of Occurrences
Establishment of student-teacher relationship	6	60%
Faculty empowerment	3	30%
Skill-based instruction	2	20%
Understanding the unique needs of students		
Students' accountability	2	20%
Job placement after college	2	20%
Appreciation of regional differences	2	20%
Campus employment	2	20%
Access to students' data	2	20%

9. Ways to engage students in the campus. In addition to the implementation of retention programs for at-risk students, I examined how the institution tried to engage students who were considering abandoning their studies. These attempts make up Category 9: (a) implementation of co-curricular activities, (b) use of technology, (c) understanding the life circumstances of students, (d) offering professional experiences, (e) personal knowledge of students, (f) offering support services, and (g) advertising campus activities. Of these seven themes, co-curricular activities and the use of technology emerged as the most implemented methods to ensure student engagement. P3-HPL remembered the ways that traditional students were engaged via co-curricular activities:

> That's one area that's really changed a lot. Early on, when I first started with the campus, we had a lot of full-time students, day-time students, [and] younger students. They would come to class and then hang out afterwards and be involved in a lot of different clubs. We had a lot of different clubs. We would have Spring fairs and so forth with lights and popcorn machines and all that traditional type of stuff. We have not had

that. As enrollment's been declining, we have not really had the population to support the clubs, plus they'd come mostly at night. They could be rushing here right after work, and they don't stick around for clubs.

As such, co-curricular activities for nontraditional students must be redefined to include activities that support students' professional advancement. As P4-HPL stated:

> For example, [in] the engineering discipline, we have the IEEE which is the International Electronics Engineering Association. What we try to do is we try to connect activities that are IEEE-related outside of the classroom for the students so the time that is spent here, they feel like they're getting the most value. For example we may have a guest speaker come in to speak to our EET students or Electronics Engineering Students and talk about a topic that they're covering in one of their classrooms to give them a better understanding of the topic, but also to have them understand better and see better what their career fields could potentially be like. We don't offer rock climbing. We don't offer fraternities. We don't have a football team. Our focus in terms of social activities outside of the classroom is more geared towards professional associations.

To define effective co-curricular activities for non-traditional students, P6-HPL recommended organizing sessions that clarify students' interests in activities:

> We've had some student forums to try to get feedback on what kinds of activities students would actually participate in. We are restarting a couple of our student organizations around engineering, as well as the Honor Society, and we're looking to try to set up

some common spaces so that students can have a gathering place that goes beyond just a study room.

Table 10: *Thematic Category 9. Ways to Engage Students in the Campus*

Themes	# of Occurrences	% of Occurrences
Co-curricular activities	6	60%
Use of technology	4	30%
Understand life circumstances	2	20%
Offers professional experiences	2	20%
Personal knowledge of students	2	20%
Offerings support services	2	20%
Advertisement of campus activities	2	20%

10. Best practices for student retention. According to the participants, best practices for student retention include: (a) student engagement, (b) establishment of support services, (c) screening incoming students, (d) providing intervention, (e) monitoring students, (f) active communication, (g) identification of at-risk students, (h) student orientation, (i) understanding students' needs, (j) professional development, (k) faculty commitment, and (l) establishment of teacher-student relationships. Of these, student engagement was by far the most identified effective approach for student retention. Seven participants believed that students' decision to drop out from a program is a function of their disengagement with the campus environment. P4-HPL stated that faculty can ensure that students are "connected to the classroom in some way with some of the social activities like we talked about with the professional associations." He emphasized the "family environment" that his campus has adopted to ensure that students remain engaged throughout the duration of the program.

Participants also looked to student engagement as an indicator of student-teacher relationships. P7-LPL claimed that when students were engaged, the faculty could "establish a more personal and individual" relationship with them. He stated that when this teacher-student relationship was strengthened, the faculty "could adapt a classroom curriculum that meet students' needs and outcome that are valuable to them." Furthermore:

Once in the classroom, each and every faculty member must feel as if they are not simply there to deliver information. If it's not an environment where the students are there to sit at their feet and obtain whatever knowledge they can glean and then go out into the world and apply it. It's incumbent upon the faculty members to ensure that the students are engaged, that they're interested in the material and that they perceive it to be meaningful for them and their personal careers.

P9-LPL believed that the disengagement of students was based on how faculty members connected with the students:

Best practices would begin in the classroom because the teachers are who these students spend the majority of their time with. If you're having issues with engagement, then faculty needs to be mentored. People need to be monitoring the shells, the classrooms, making sure that everyone is following best practices for teaching and engaging the students in the classroom, both physically and online.

Table 11 shows other best practices mentioned by participants. These practices have important functions, but were often criticized as not feasible given the declining number of students at the university.

Table 11: *Thematic Category 10. Best Practices for Student Retention in Private For-Profit Institutions*

Themes	# of Occurrences	% of Occurrences
Student engagement	7	70%
Establishment of support group	3	30%
Establishment of student-teacher relationship	3	30%
Providing intervention	2	20%
Monitoring of students	2	20%
Active communication	2	20%
Identification of at-risk students	2	20%
Students' orientation	1	10%
Understanding students' challenges	1	10%
Professional development trainings for teachers	1	10%
Committed faculties	1	10%

Conclusions

When examining the information given by the participants in this study, it becomes clear that faculty and administrators from high- and low-retention campuses have very different outlooks, even when they are part of the same university system. Although it is hard to generalize these observations to other groups due to the small sample utilized in the study, two major dichotomies come to light: services rendered versus relationships built and external incentives versus internal motivations. Among faculty and administrators from low-persistence campuses, the participants emphasized the importance of academic and other services available to students. Contrarily, the high-persistence campuses were more likely to focus their energies on developing ongoing relationships with both current students and alumni. The remainder of this section will explore these differences before moving in Part 4 to examine factors that influence retention from the student perspective.

Services rendered versus relationships built. For-profit schools often struggle with an image of lower academic quality than public or non-profit institutions. Whether or not this is a fair image, current popular discourse paints these institutions as significantly lacking in both academic standards and accountability. Thanks to open (or at least less restrictive) admissions standards, for-profit colleges and universities serve a far more diverse student body with a wide range of backgrounds, experiences, and skill-sets. This often presents a challenge for retention and completion rates: unlike their traditional counterparts, teachers and administrators at for-profit schools cannot assume that students enter with the academic, social, or life skills that facilitate success in postsecondary education. Furthermore, the very flexibility and innovation that helps for-profit colleges and universities to flourish—serving students in different life stages, flexible scheduling, distance and online learning—often makes it difficult to implement an effective system of academic accountability. This, in turn, may lead to students "falling through the cracks"—losing sight of their academic goals or their overall progress.

Even with these challenges, the question of student retention is extremely important to for-profit institutions, possibly even more so than for traditional colleges and universities. Student graduation and retention rates often function as a proxy for academic quality, particularly among potential students and government regulators. Legislative and policy discussions about for-profit colleges and universities often center on the number of students who complete their degrees within a reasonable timeframe. Similarly, both potential students and government entities look at the jobs that graduates receive, with particular attention focused on the number of graduates employed within their desired fields. Alumni provide a major source of employment opportunities for a school's graduates, and problems with student completion affect both the strength and the effectiveness of alumni networks for future student employment. Finally, achieving high completion levels is often an issue of existential importance for private and for-profit institutions. Whereas public/non-profit schools can rely on government programs, private grants, research monies, and robust alumni funding for a significant portion of their revenues, the operating budgets of for-profit schools depend almost exclusively on tuition and fees from students.

Given the importance of the issue, student retention was naturally very high on the list of concerns for faculty and administrators at both high- and low-persistence campuses. However, their understanding of the problem and its solutions diverged very sharply. Administrators from low-persistence campuses talked a great deal about academic services offered. The LPL participants often pointed to concrete offerings like academic tutoring, technological support, course offerings, and facilities. They also noted the presence of mandatory communication between faculty and at-risk students, though they often claimed that this was unhelpful to student retention.

Those from high-persistence locations, on the other hand, discussed ways of building two-way relationships with at-risk students as well as alumni. At high-persistence campuses, faculty and administrators also noted the structures that they had built to help students succeed and complete their degrees, but these campuses seemed to have more success with their strategies of communicating with high-risk students. While the low-persistence administrators emphasized the mandatory nature of such contact, high-persistence campuses tended to integrate this contact into co-curricular activities, job placement programs, and alumni engagement. The success of this kind of relationship building supports Tinto's (1993) earlier findings, which stated that only 20-30% of students who dropped out did so for academic reasons. The rest, he claimed, left college for a variety of other reasons, including a general sense of investment, fitting in, and the existence of a meaningful relationship between the institution and the student. Finding organic, non-coercive, and mutually useful ways of strengthening the connection between students and the university at every level of interaction can go a long way towards helping students persist to graduation.

External versus internal motivation. While the issue of building relationships between an institution and its students is, to a large extent, within a school's control, the second major difference between high-persistence campuses and low-persistence campuses is not: the question of student motivation. This may partially explain why low-persistence campuses focused their attention mostly on academic milestones and goals, largely ignoring qualities like student motivation, life skills, or character traits. Although this is in line with the focus of government regulators and policymakers, it does not correlate well with students actually finishing their degrees. High-persistence campuses, on the other hand, took a more holistic approach to achieving and maintaining students' overall engagement with school by packaging elements such as extra- and co-curricular activities, advising and mentorship, internships and job placement, and alumni contact. These approaches helped to bolster and enhance the trait of intrinsic motivation, an important element of student persistence and degree completion.

Rather than constantly requiring outside affirmation in their pursuits, intrinsically motivated students generate the desire to persist from their own feelings of engagement with their goals. Multiple previous studies have indicated that intrinsic motivation is an important element of student persistence and degree completion. Although it may at first seem difficult to teach a trait or life orientation, there are some steps that schools can take to improve student motivation. By tailoring services to students' needs rather than to academic goals, schools can help students to develop an independent investment in the educational process instead of viewing the school as a set of requirements to be fulfilled. Following Tinto's (1993) lead, schools can also enhance motivation and persistence by creating more effective relationships, particularly between students and teachers. The faculty-student relationship is an invaluable part of the educational process, and it can also help prevent the non-academic dropouts that Tinto claimed represented the majority of student failures to finish degrees.

Given these conclusions, in the fourth section of this book, I examine the issue of student persistence from the student perspective, outlining factors that influence student success in three main areas: the transition to college/university life, managing school work, and student mental health. Here, I aim to equip educators and administrators with a set of general principles to understand the student experience better in their diverse institutional environments—whether nonprofit or for-profit, public or private. This discussion also aims to provide students with information to make sure that they are well prepared and equipped to succeed in college/university. This discussion is followed by a synthesis of the various perspectives, which provide a set of recommendations for improving student retention in higher education institutions.

Part Four

Cultivating the Persistent Student

In this book so far, I have discussed the issues affecting student retention in higher education primarily from the perspective of the institution (i.e., administration and faculty). In the final section of this book, I approach this topic from another vital perspective: that of the student. Key to this discussion is the assertion that understanding the issues students face is key to cultivating student persistence, as is understanding the essential qualities that persistent students tend to possess. Such an understanding can then be utilized to inform policy development as well as programming aimed at increasing student retention and improving student and institutional outcomes not only in the for-profit institution, but also for all higher education institutions. Generally, when students possess strong coping skills to manage the stress and demands of university programs in addition to their daily lives, then they will be more responsive to institutional efforts to increase student retention. Additionally, knowledge of these issues may help students themselves to identify potential risk factors that may affect their persistence throughout their time in school, providing them with the first step to better their chances of completing their education. It may also encourage students to locate and utilize a variety of institutional services and resources that may help to increase their chances of success (e.g., peer mentoring services, mental health services, transition interventions), and to develop the personal and professional relationships that will further support them throughout their time in college. As such, in order to unpack this complex issue, here I focus on three main areas or factors that broadly impact student success, identifying some of the traits or skills that help students to be persistent: (a) the transition to university life, (b) managing schoolwork, and (c) student mental health.

The Challenge of Persistence: The Student Perspective

As discussed throughout this book, student persistence is an issue facing all types of educational institutions in today's fast-paced, global environment. This is true of both traditional brick-and-mortar institutions (private, non-profit, and state-funded), as well as for the newer online education programs that have rapidly increased in enrollment in recent years. Indeed, student persistence is an issue that crosses all disciplinary boundaries and organizational types, pointing to the widespread social and economic implications that stem from school leavers. In previous sections, I have explained the issue of student retention primarily in relation to the institutional level (i.e., relating to administration, staff, and faculty). While institutional factors and interventions highly impact retention, as I have shown, there is also a set of issues specifically related to the student experience that must be understood in order to explicate the problem of student retention fully.

From the student perspective, there are a number of factors that impact students' ability to complete their studies. Students must maintain a positive work–life balance, juggling family, schoolwork, and often employment, which can range from part-time work on campus to full-time work outside of the student's institution. Students must also cope with a new social environment that may be outside of their comfort zone and previous realm of experience, as well as the demands of schoolwork that requires skills they may not readily possess or have acquired in their previous life experience/education. On top of this, many students also face immense financial pressure from the cost of study, and an alarming number of students now face large student debt. It is no surprise, then, that students struggle to be persistent in their studies. Fortunately, there are strategies that can improve student retention not only from the institutional perspective but also on a more individual level. Overall, in the following discussion, I show how students can manage some of the systemic challenges they face to be successful in school, and how institutions can respond to student needs to improve student retention.

The Transition to College Life

Transitioning to college life is a significant adjustment for many students. Students must adapt to a new environment where, possibly for the first time, they are in a new place surrounded by new people. They may be leaving home for the first time, relocating to a new city, and entering new social circles. Consequently, students may be leaving their comfort zones and support networks, including leaving friends and family. Even in online schools or when students stay in their hometowns—regardless of age—students must adapt to new demands on their time, finances, and energy, and work to develop new social and professional networks. This includes forming new relationships with peers, faculty, and staff, and navigating new social circles as the 'new kid on the block.' At the same time, students must learn to meet a new set of expectations that exceeds their previous academic experience and develop a new set of skills to succeed in university coursework, while navigating the bureaucracy of university administration. In these ways, when students enter college, they are entering the unknown, and are forced to navigate what may be an overwhelming, confusing process of change. The transition to college is thus as an important time for setting students' foundation for success, for building the essentials skills and tools students will utilize throughout their college careers. It is also a time for students to set clear academic goals and to develop a plan to achieve those goals.

This transition may be more challenging for students who are underprepared for college (as seen through such indicators as SAT scores and high school grades) or who are the first in their families to attend college, and therefore do not have role models, familial support, or access to insider knowledge of the college experience (Holliday, 2014). For these students especially, programs aimed at college readiness and adjustment may help to increase success and student retention, providing essential skills, tips, and tricks to succeed in the college environment as well as social support. Indeed, for all students, addressing college adjustment is especially important as students who adjust well to college life achieve higher educational outcomes and are more likely to meet their goals (Holliday, 2014). In the following sections, I specify three areas of focus or engagement, which may help students during their transition to college: (a) work–life balance, (b) socialization, and (c) involvement in on-campus activities. Developing strategies to address these three areas both at the institutional and individual levels is key to helping students adjust to college life successfully.

Work–life balance. A key aspect of succeeding in the college environment is understanding what it takes to achieve a balance between an individual's personal and professional lives, or the "work–life balance." This includes both managing academic coursework with the additional and often external work many students do to support themselves and their education, as well as managing the demands of school and work with the demands of their families and social lives. Many students may feel that to be successful in school or their careers, they have to sacrifice their family or social life. For example, a student may feel they cannot attend a family function because they need to study, or on a larger level, may have to postpone starting a family of their own until they finish school. This can make schoolwork feel onerous and isolating, divorcing students from much-needed social support.

As Tan-Wilson and Stamp (2015) have noted, "research recognizes that work and personal life domains can impact one another in positive and negative ways" (p. 2). For example, students that dedicate all of their time to studying may feel they are sacrificing time with their friends and family, and those relationships may suffer. This is especially true in situations where a student's family and/or friends have not been through a college program and are unable to understand and empathize with the student's workload. Alternatively, students that prioritize meeting family demands may not be able to prepare fully for classwork. Students with large family responsibilities (e.g., parents, those supporting family members) may have little flexibility in their schedules and demands on their time. It is important for students to realize that maintaining a good work–life balance means being flexible to adapt to the changing demands of their personal and professional domains over time, and learning how to prioritize effectively in order to satisfy requirements in both areas. It is also important for institutions to understand the demands that students have outside of the college environment in order to be able to provide support that meets students' needs effectively. For example, the provision of affordable on-campus childcare options or financial childcare subsidies may help students who are parents to meet the demands of their coursework better—thus improving their work–life balance— by reducing the time spent and costs associated with childcare.

Practically, achieving a work–life balance also requires good time management and communication skills. Learning to use time effectively and efficiently helps students to balance often-conflicting demands and to schedule their priorities accordingly, in a way that works for their unique situation. Communicating clearly with family and friends about school requirements and timelines helps those in a student's social network to understand the demands being placed upon him/her and, in turn, to support the student to achieve those goals. Overall, achieving a work–life balance ensures that students can meet their educational goals while receiving social support and lowering the stress of multiple demands—all factors that enhance student persistence.

Socialization. Recent evidence on student retention shows that "the degree of the student's social integration in the campus community influences the level of commitment during the academic journey and thus the likelihood of successfully completing that journey" (Gilardi & Guglielmetti, 2011, p. 35). Feeling secure, comfortable, integrated, and socially connected in the college environment promotes retention behavior in students, and helps them to take ownership over their college journey and goals. Robbins, Oh, Le, and Button (2009) argued that engagement in social networks (both formal and informal) helps students develop and maintain a sense of relatedness and embeddedness in the college environment. This engagement can be broadly conceptualized as a process of socialization, where students learn to navigate the social environment of the institution and develop their own personal and professional social networks. On an individual level, it is important for students to understand the vital role social connection plays in providing an academic and personal support system that will help them succeed in college. While some students may find it difficult to enter a new social environment, participation in campus programming aimed at socialization may help to ease the transition.

Socialization can be encouraged through institutional interventions including freshman orientation programs for incoming college students and First Year Experience programming, which implements socialization strategies over the course of a semester or year (Robbins, Oh, Le, & Button, 2009). It can also be accomplished through community-building activities that continue throughout students' college careers (e.g., mentorship programs, student groups, social events, etc.), as well as via participation in a variety of on-campus activities, as further discussed below.

It is important to note that students enrolled in online programs may face additional challenges in the transition process due to their minimal access to a social environment that provides support. More so than traditional brick-and-mortar schools, online schools must take additional measures to ensure that students interact with each other as such interaction may not be as intuitive, meaningful, or engaging for students from the outset than face-to-face socialization. This is especially true for those who are new to online social networking processes or the use of online technology in education.

On-campus involvement. Following from the need for socialization discussed above, participation on campus helps students to transition more easily to college life by providing a means for them to engage directly in the college environment. Such engagement helps students develop new social networks more quickly, and helps them feel a part of and included in the college environment, which is key to the socialization process as well as the transition process overall. As Holliday (2014) notes, the degree of a student's involvement on campus is directly tied to and impacts his/her development and retention (p. 27).

Fortunately, there are many options for on-campus involvement in most institutions. Such options may range from extracurricular activities in athletics and the performing arts, to student-led study groups, to a range of student clubs and interest groups, to religious or ethnic associations, to fraternity/sorority groups, to on-campus employment and service/volunteering opportunities. It is important for students to identify which options suit their schedules and preferences early on, so they may take advantage of all the opportunities for on-campus involvement that suit them. It is also important, however, for students to be realistic regarding the time and energy they have to devote to such activities, so that it does not interfere with their overall ability to manage their time and/or become a stressor.

While students may initially feel that engaging in on-campus activities in addition to their coursework may increase the demands of an already full schedule, such participation may provide necessary stress relief and social connection, improving overall mental health and focus, and reducing feelings of isolation. Athletic participation, for example (as in all exercise), has been widely shown to have a myriad of physical and cognitive benefits, including lowering stress, increasing mental stamina, increasing endurance, and improving sleep. Both lower stress and improved sleep have been shown to improve academic performance, in turn increasing retention. Therefore, by increasing the overall wellbeing of the student as a whole, such participation increases the student's ability to succeed in all aspects of life, therefore bettering the student's chance of success in school.

Managing Schoolwork

As Landek (2013) has shown, "the interaction between students' attributes, skills, and dispositions, along with the institution's academic and social systems, are key factors in the discussion of student persistence" (p. 139). As such, in the remainder of Part 4, I outline some of these attributes, skills, and dispositions to understand better what factors influence retention from the student perspective. I begin by identifying four areas students should consider when developing strategies to manage their schoolwork effectively: (a) study skills, (b) time management, (c) procrastination, and (d) technology. I then move on to a discussion of student mental health in the final sections, examining the more psychological aspects of student retention, including stress, self-esteem, motivation, and self-efficacy.

Study skills. Effective and efficient study skills are an essential building block for college success. *Study skills* are those skills required to complete academic assignments and tasks successfully, such as goal setting, time management, note-taking, memorization, reading comprehension, self-testing, and critical thinking. Study skills must be developed through study habits and patterns that work for the individual student, as each student has specific learning needs and styles (Lei, 2015). Physical location, atmosphere, time of day, duration, social company, use of resources, study technique, study ability/aptitude for learning, and learning style are all factors that must be taken into consideration to create the optimal study environment and pattern for each individual student.

Often, students learn what works best for them through trial and error during their transition period. It is important to note that many students may be underprepared or not prepared for college, and may lack the skills they need to cope with and succeed in adjusting to college. As a result, many first-year institutional programs also now offer tutorials or course components that teach study skills to their students, including such topics as how to read and discern information from scholarly resources, how to use the library, how to conduct literature searches, and how to prepare notes for classes and exams. These courses may also include training in basic literacy and writing skills. Overall, establishing positive and effective study habits early on is important for students, as these habits will inform how they complete their work throughout the rest of their college careers.

While "what works best" varies from student to student, there are some general attributes that are common to students who are academically successful. Lei (2015) stated that most students should allow two hours of studying per classroom hour (including homework and research), ideally between breakfast and dinner. Regularly scheduling these study hours daily help students to allocate the time needed for each task and avoid procrastination. Students should also take frequent short study breaks to relax and refresh their minds. In terms of location, students need to identify what location suits their preferences and needs—their dorm room, a coffee shop, the library—and avoid places that are fraught with distractions. For some students, variation in the environment helps to keep their minds active; for others the same location helps to build strong study habits (Lei, 2015). Again, the importance here is for students to understand not what works generally, but what works specifically for them.

From an institutional perspective, professors need to understand the importance of helping students to develop strong study skills, habits, and patterns. One study (Tuckman & Kennedy, 2011) found that in a program where first-year students took a course based on educational psychology where they identified learning strategies and learned study skills, the students' graduation rates were 50% higher for students who were initially experiencing academic difficulty. Study skill development may thus play a significant role in increasing student success and retention.

Time management. While time management can be considered a study skill, it warrants further discussion as "student time is a valuable resource, and student success is related to the investment of time and effort by the student" (Landek, 2013, p. 141). Effective time management influences students' ability to manage academic coursework, to maintain a work–life balance, and to avoid procrastination. As such, there are many factors in successful time management. Students must take into consideration their learning/study needs and styles (i.e., the time they take to complete academic tasks), their academic and real-life demands (e.g., deadlines, work schedules, family obligations, etc.), the time required to participate in on-campus activities, and logistical aspects such as transportation time. Having a realistic picture of these demands and allocating reasonable amounts of time to complete each task is key to developing a sustainable schedule.

In today's digital era, there are many calendar, to-do list, and organizer apps that may help students with time management. However, in order for these kinds of resources to be successful, students must be open to developing and sticking to a routine. Students must also accept responsibility for and take ownership over their schedules. This is particularly important for non-traditional students who are balancing additional external demands and/or are learning online, where accountability is almost entirely independently led. With good planning, realistic expectations, and a strong commitment, however, good time management skills will ease stress and help students to achieve their academic goals.

Procrastination. One of the biggest challenges that many students have is how to manage tendencies toward procrastination, which can be understood as willfully delaying an action until it is absolutely necessary. Rather than completing school-related actions (e.g., selecting courses, completing paperwork, working on assignments) when they are first assigned or through a slow-and-steady approach (where students work on tasks gradually over a set period of time), procrastinators tend to wait until the last minute to complete tasks.

Procrastination has important implications in all aspects of students' lives, even in areas that may be less obvious for students. Most students understand that failing to work on an assignment until the eleventh hour will likely sacrifice the quality of their work on that assignment or their ability to complete it by the deadline. However, some students (especially first-year students) may not consider procrastination's impacts on other areas such as in administrative or logistical matters or the availability of on-campus involvement. Take, for example, the impact of procrastination on enrollment. For students in institutions that may be overcrowded, there may be high amounts of competition to enroll in certain courses as there are larger numbers of students than can be accommodated in a particular course (Gurantz, 2015). In such a case, delaying registration to the last minute may highly impact the courses available to the student, directly impacting his/her learning and ability to achieve course requirements within their intended timeframe as well as his/her overall college goals. Additionally, not being able to enroll in the courses of a student's choosing may impact his/her motivation and engagement within the courses he/she does take, impacting the student's academic success and overall retention in the program. As Gurantz (2015) wrote, "the mechanism that predicts whether late registrants persist is whether they were able to eventually enroll in a meaningful number of courses" (p. 526).

There are many strategies and resources that may help to manage or reduce tendencies toward procrastination. Targeted organization and planning here are particularly important. First and foremost, as with general time management skills, keeping an up-to-date calendar with deadlines clearly outlined is essential. Breaking up larger tasks (e.g., an assignment) into smaller units of action or "action steps" and scheduling these actions over a period of time (e.g., allotting a certain amount of actions per day until the deadline) may help students to work more gradually and to avoid trying to rush through large amounts of work in a small timeframe. Here, the student can also create additional deadlines for these actions in addition to the deadline for the overall task, which helps create a sense of accountability for the student. For those who require extra help, setting these partial deadlines with a study buddy, teaching assistant, or professor may create the additional accountability needed to achieve the goal.

Technology. With the wide adoption of technology within the classroom in recent decades, students must adjust not only to the traditional demands of coursework (reading, writing, studying, etc.) but must also develop technological skills to be able to utilize online resources such as library databases as well as online course platforms such as Blackboard. For those students who are completing their education through online universities, this need to adapt to technological requirements is even more essential to their success. And yet, online students may lack the initial resources and know-how to utilize such technology effectively. This may be challenging especially for older non-traditional students who have not grown up fully immersed in technology. Fortunately, most institutions offer tutorials and one-on-one help to navigate the technology utilized in the school, most often through the library. It is important for institutions to emphasize the availability of these resources, and to encourage students to make use of them. Similarly, taking advantage of said resources is likely to increase the ease, comfort level, and efficiency for students' use of technology.

Additionally, as previously discussed, there are a number of software programs and apps that students may find useful to help their schoolwork, from time management and calendar apps, to to-do list apps, to flashcard and memorization apps, to note-taking software, to database and citation software, to apps that block an individual's access from certain websites or apps (e.g., Facebook) for a certain period of time. While students may have varying access to technology, most institutions provide library access so that students may, at the very least, have access to computers on a regular basis. And, as institutions now generally require that students utilize computer resources to complete assignments, students generally possess higher levels of technological literacy. This means that utilizing technological resources to support positive study habits should be an easy step to adopt for most students. Making use of these resources to suit each individual's unique needs may provide useful support for students as they work to develop their study skills and habits.

Student Mental Health

Research has shown that many students grapple with mental health issues throughout their college careers (Mandracchia & Pendleton, 2015). While prevalence rates tend to vary, it is estimated that almost half of all college students generally fit the criteria for a mental disorder (Hunt & Eisenberg, 2010). Indeed, in one study of 1,033 college students (Laughlin & Robinson, 2004), the researchers found that "one out of seven students reported that mental health problems were interfering with their daily functioning at college, one third reported ongoing feelings of depression, and one fourth reported feelings of suicidal ideation" (Nordstrom, Swenson Goguen, & Hiester, 2014, p. 48). At the same time, many college students engage in "disproportionately high levels" of maladaptive, risky, or dangerous behaviors such as excessive or binge drinking or 'experimentation' with illicit drugs (Mandracchia & Pendleton, 2015, p. 227–228). However, despite these common issues, in keeping with society more broadly, students typically underutilize health and mental health services at their institutions, and often fail to report or seek treatment for their issues. As a result, these students may proceed in their college work without the institutional, medical, or social support they need to manage their issues, lowering their chances for success and consequently increasing their likelihood of failure.

The issues of retention and student mental health are deeply intertwined. The majority of students—roughly 70%—who utilize mental health resources at university counseling centers report the negative impact their mental health issues have on their academic performance; with up to 20% contemplating leaving school due to their problems (Turner & Berry, 2000, as cited in Mandracchia & Pendleton, 2015, p. 227). Interestingly, mental health issues seem to affect more of those students who are already at a higher risk of academic failure and leaving school. For example, research has shown that mental health is of particular concern during students' transition to college, as students enter a new developmental period of "emerging adulthood" marked by instability, insecurity, and change (Mandracchia & Pendleton, 2015; Zaddach, 2013). Consequently, as Zaddach (2013) noted, "first-year students are disproportionally more vulnerable to emotional maladjustment and mental health concerns, and are at higher risk for academic failure" (p. 1). First-generation students also experience higher rates of mental distress and illness than non-first-generation students (Stebleton, Soria, & Huesman, 2014), possibly due to their lack of insider resources to understand the college environment and social support, further in keeping with statistics regarding student retention.

Due to the interconnected relationship between student mental health and retention, in order to improve students' chances of success, organizations must provide students with resources to support their emotional and mental health (Zaddach, 2013). While counseling centers and hotlines are available on most campuses, these resources are often underutilized by students for a number of reasons including personal denial or lack of understanding of the mental health issue, a lack of familiarity or comfort with university health services, and most notably, the stigma of seeking mental health treatment. Instead, most students turn to individuals already in their social support networks to support them, instead of seeking professional help (Merianos, Nabors, Vidourek, & King, 2013). However, in many cases these individuals may not be able to offer the amount and type of help required, due to their own limitations (e.g., lack of training, knowledge, time, etc.). It is thus important for institutions to incorporate education outreach such as mental health awareness campaigns as a part of their efforts in this domain. College campus staff and faculty are in a unique position to reach students at the time they may need it the most, in order to help prevent mental disorders among college students and to increase the amount of students who seek professional treatment (Merianos et al., 2013). In the remainder of Part 4, I discuss four areas pertaining to mental health that have been shown to particularly impact retention: (a) stress, (b) self-esteem, (c) motivation, and (d) self-efficacy. While a broader understanding of mental health issues would likely benefit both the education institution and its students more generally, my goal here is to provide students (and institutions) with an awareness of these key factors so they may adopt strategies that particularly impact their likeliness to succeed in college.

Stress. As Hurst, Baranik, and Daniel (2012) pointed out, research examining student stressors is very important. In today's college environment, students face increasing academic, social, and financial pressures. For example, the cost of tuition, room, and board has increased 37% in the last decade alone (Hurst, Baranik, & Daniel, 2012, p. 275). Without an adequate means to cope with stress, students may experience negative impacts on their overall physical and psychological health and wellbeing. It is no wonder then, that the degree to which students experience stress directly affects their persistence in school (Johnson, Wasserman, Yildirim, & Yonai, 2014). Ford (2014) found that as students' stress level increases, they become less likely to graduate. In contrast, students with good emotional health are more likely to graduate (De Angelo et al., 2011, as cited in Johnson et al., 2014, p. 76). In one study, as much as 25% of college students indicated that stress is a leading factor in their academic performance, with 39% stating they had experienced higher than average amounts of stress within the past year (American College Health Association, 2011, as cited in Johnson et al., 2014, p. 76).

Such stress may result from a variety of factors, from the university transition, to financial pressures, to examinations, to students' personal lives (Hurst et al., 2012). Consequently, it is likely that all students will experience a degree of stress during their college careers. At the institutional level, Hurst et al. (2012) argued that faculty, administrators, and staff such as student health center employees and internship advisors should help to "create opportunities for students to manage stress" (p. 282), such as encouraging meaningful faculty–student interactions, teaching stress management in the classroom, and providing 'soft skills' training for students. These interventions and programs should take into account the unique needs of the student body, along with the particular concerns facing minority students, first-generation students, and students with disabilities. For students themselves, it is very important to understand what their individual stressors are and how they are affected by stress, and to learn tools to cope with their stress. From exercise, to mediation, to spirituality, to counseling, there are many tools available to students both on and off campus that may help reduce and/or relieve their stress. Without acknowledging their stressors and taking responsibility for their mental health—including dealing with stress—students may lack the resources and know-how to overcome the challenges they face to persist in college.

Self-esteem. *Self-esteem* is "an evaluative form of a person's self-representation" that is "highly affected by domain and development" (Nordstrom et al., 2014, p. 50). Rather than simply a person's idea of his/her overall self-worth or sense of self, self-esteem as a broader concept is quite complex. A whole set of ideas or notions about the individual self and his/her various competencies in different areas make up self-esteem, including such areas as social skills, academic skills, athletic skills, physical appearance, and attractiveness. The combination of these ideas creates a tapestry or profile that constitutes the individual's self-esteem, where the individual possesses strengths and weaknesses in different areas (Nordstrom et al.,

2014). Self-esteem is affected by a number of factors including the individual's mental health, social upbringing, and level of self-confidence.

Self-esteem is an important part of a student's overall and general mental health. As Merianos, Nabors, Vidourek, and King (2013) explained, "self-esteem and social-support are interrelated concepts that serve as protective factors against developing mental health problems during the college years" (p. 28). In one study (Merianos et al., 2013), the authors found that students with lower self-esteem would be more likely to have lower academic performance and achievement goals, as well as "poorer grades, decreased emotional skills, social isolation, and financial issues" (p. 32), which may ultimately lead to lower GPAs and decreased student retention.

Nordstrom et al. (2014) asserted that "self-esteem appears to be a worthy target of treatment" (p. 59) at the institutional level, particularly for first-semester students who are in the transition period. The authors suggested that such treatment could include pairing students with peer leaders, as research has shown building such relationships helps to increase persistence, satisfaction, and feelings of belonging. From the student perspective, it is important that they understand how their sense of self-worth, self-esteem, and self-efficacy may impact their success in college. This is especially true for female students, as they are more likely to experience low levels of self-esteem than male students (Merianos et al., 2013). Because acknowledging self-esteem is an issue may be daunting to some students, good social and institutional support is essential for students to reduce stigmatization and increase their likelihood to seek treatment.

Motivation. *Motivation* can be defined as the desire to achieve a goal, or "to be moved to do something" (Ryan & Deci, 2000, p. 54). Contrarily, an unmotivated person is someone who "feels no impetus or inspiration to act" (Ryan & Deci, 2000, p. 54). In the educational psychology literature, following Ryan and Deci's (1985) early work in Self-Determination Theory, motivation is typically divided into two types: intrinsic and extrinsic. *Intrinsic motivation* is when an individual does something "because it is inherently interesting or enjoyable" to them (e.g., because a student likes the assignment), and *extrinsic motivation* is when the individual chooses to do something because "it leads to a separable outcome," for example to gain the approval of a teacher or due to peer pressure (Ryan & Deci, 2000, p. 55). Everyone has a different amount or *level* of motivation, along with different kinds or *orientations* of motivation (Ryan & Deci, 2000); in order to understand motivation we must consider both of these factors.

Ryan and Deci (2000) argued that motivation deeply impacts student success. Of the two kinds, intrinsic motivation is generally regarded as more beneficial for students, as it "results in high-quality learning and creativity" and increase persistence (Ryan & Deci, 2000, p. 55). It is also likely that higher levels of intrinsic motivation may help to reduce or buffer mental health issues, as intrinsic motivation is linked to feelings of happiness and satisfaction—students who enjoy their time in school are more likely to have a positive experience.

In terms of college students, as is the case more generally, a high level of motivation among students is noted as a predictor of overall college success and retention (Witting, n.d.). A student's level of motivation is directly tied to many aspects of a student's life, such as goal setting and attainment, mental health, and the issue of procrastination. For example, students who are less intrinsically or self-motivated to succeed in college and achieve their goals may be more likely to procrastinate in accomplishing school-related work. Similarly, students who are dissatisfied or feel coerced within their programs to achieve goals that they do not own or feel resonate with them may be more likely to resist such goals, or may feel more stress in completing the tasks required to achieve the goals.

There are many factors that impact college students' motivation (both intrinsic and extrinsic), including overall academic skills and achievement, overall enjoyment in school, social support, external stressors such as financial burdens, and personal goals. Unsurprisingly, research has shown that students who feel they are not in the right program for them, are bored in their coursework, or feel their course(s) and/or program do not suit their skills and interests are more likely to leave school (Witting, n.d.). For these reasons, at the institutional level, it is important for educators to adopt strategies to increase student motivation. For students, again understanding is key: students must have a clear idea of what their motivations and goals are in order to choose the courses, program, school, and study habits that will foster their success in college.

Self-efficacy. Another concept closely linked to students' self-esteem, motivation, and overall success is *self-efficacy*, or a student's "belief in one's capabilities to organize and execute courses of action required to produce given attainments" (Bandura, 1997, p. 3, as cited in Chemers, Hu, & Garcia, 2001, p. 55). Students' sense of self-efficacy impacts the choices they make in college, their sense of self-confidence, how much effort they put into their work, their ability to persevere in the face of challenges, their level of resilience, and their ability to cope with stressors (Chemers et al., 2001). Consequently, self-efficacy is highly connected to students' mental health, academic performance, and persistence.

Chemers, Hu, and Garcia (2001) described three processes that are mediated by self-efficacy effects in relation to educational achievement: (a) cognitive processes, (b) motivational processes, and (c) affective processes. In the first area, increased self-efficacy impacts a student's confidence in his/her ability to achieve a goal or problem solve effectively. This may include navigating the complex environment of the institution, and comprehending and revising knowledge based on feedback and testing, along with metacognitive strategies such as planning and self-regulation. In relation to retention, students who have high self-efficacy "make greater use of cognitive strategies in learning, manage their time and learning environments more effectively, and are better at monitoring and regulating their own effort" (p. 56). This leads to higher academic achievement and persistence.

In the second area, motivational processes, Chemers et al. (2001) explained the positive impacts of self-efficacy on motivation, where increased self-efficacy leads to better decision-making in terms of setting goals. Students are more able to judge, set, and achieve their goals, which leads to better task performance and evaluation. As the authors stated, "when goals provide a standard, highly efficacious persons show a stronger relationship among self-evaluation, self-direction, and performance" (p. 56), leading to better educational outcomes.

Finally, Chemers et al. (2001) described the third area: affective processes. This area relates directly to student mental health, and includes the impacts of students' emotions and affects on their learning, attention, adjustment, and concentration. It also influences how students respond to and cope with challenges, and their ability to find solutions to those challenges. For example, people with higher levels of self-efficacy can better manage anxiety and negative emotions such as stress, and utilize available coping resources more effectively.

Self-efficacy underpins student success more generally as higher levels of self-efficacy positively improve student mental health, academic achievement, motivation, and persistence. It is therefore important for institutions and students to adopt strategies to increase student self-efficacy, including opportunities for building peer and teacher–student relationships and mentoring, as previously suggested. Similarly, it is important for students to understand the concept of self-efficacy and how it may impact their schoolwork. Following from this discussion, in the final section of this book, I offer some brief concluding remarks and recommendations on the issue of student persistence to tie together the themes that I have highlighted throughout.

Part Five

Concluding Remarks and Recommendations for Practice

Student retention is a pressing issue facing higher education institutions in today's global economy. At for-profit institutions, for example, the completion rate has declined to 43% in recent years (National Commission on Higher Education Attainment, 2013). With students burdened with the rising costs of tuition and other stressors, coupled with increasing competition between institutions particularly due to the online education sector, dropout rates continue to soar. Retention issues affect higher education institutions and their students holistically—leading to damage to the school's reputation, networking ability, and fiscal status—making retention an important area of intervention for administrators, faculty, and students alike.

Student persistence and dropout is a complex issue affected by a number of institutional and individual factors. For example, at the institutional level, especially in this era of online distance learning, factors such as the institution's local geography, availability of funding, accessibility of student services, staffing, student population (e.g., socioeconomic status; minorities and students with disabilities; nontraditional or first-generation students) highly affect retention. From a student perspective, aspects including college preparedness, study management skills, socialization, external stressors, and mental health further impact their persistence in school.

Fortunately, some institutional efforts to increase student retention have been successful in tackling this issue. Successful interventions tend to feature collaboration among institution personnel (e.g., administrators, coordinators, advisors, supports staff, faculty) as well as between staff and students, and provide advising, mentoring, and other student support services. These are particularly effective when aimed at first-year students who are in their transition to college, as they are of the most at-risk students for college dropout. Successful programs further work to identify and meet the specific needs of the student population at the institution.

In our increasingly technological age, one particular area offering new and powerful tools to improve student retention is the field of big data analytics. Learning analytics and educational data mining, for example, provide new means to predict student success—and design retention interventions—based upon the analysis of large quantities of digital information about student records and trends. With the substantial growth of online education in recent years, a new body of data is available for institutions to learn about student behaviors through their level of engagement with online activities. This is particularly important when a large portion of online or distance learning students are members of at-risk student populations (e.g., nontraditional students, minority students, etc.). This provides institutions with a key opportunity to learn what strategies may impact this body of students the most. Indeed, in one study (Calvert, 2014), the researcher was able to create a predictive model of student success with 95% accuracy. Such analysis, however, may fail to take into account the real-life experiences of students. Therefore, big data analytics may be best utilized by institutions in concert with research stemming from other methodologies that focus on students' and educators' perspectives.

Indeed, at the heart of this issue is the experience of the students themselves while they are in college, along with their ability to cope with their experiences. In Part 4, I discussed how the transition to college is an important time for both traditional and nontraditional college students, where they face new challenges and stressors, and enter a new social environment and professional network. Students must also adjust to the expectations and demands of academic coursework, and learn new study skills including time management, how to avoid procrastination, and how to adapt to the technological demands of school. Because of these transitional changes and the general demands of college, students may experience new or increased mental health issues, which may directly affect their daily functioning while in school both during the transition period and beyond. Mental health issues including stress and self-esteem, along with students' level of motivation and self-efficacy, all impact student retention, with lower levels of stress and higher levels of self-esteem, motivation, and self-efficacy linked to increased student persistence. Following this discussion, in closing I reviewed the issue of retention first in theory, briefly noting some of the key concepts of two of the major contributors in the field of education—Tinto and Bordieu. I then turned to persistence in practice, providing a set of six recommendations to increase student retention based upon the evidence presented in this book.

Retention in Theory: Key Concepts

The issue of student retention has been examined from a number of theoretical angles. Tinto's (1993) pivotal work has taught us that academic factors are not the only reasons students fail to persist in their studies—as previously noted, up to 80% of students who leave school before completion do so for nonacademic reasons. While these factors may include aspects outside of the school environment, Tinto (1993) underscored that the social and academic environment—including the school's value system—are key to the students' ability to adjust to college and therefore succeed in their studies. This means that we must consider all of the aspects of students' lives as well as the institution itself to understand student persistence fully.

In another realm, Bordieu's (1986) ideas on human, financial, cultural, and social capital offer another explanation of factors that affect student retention. For example, a lack of or diminished financial capital may mean students struggle to manage the increasing demands of college tuition (and debt), leading to stress that negatively impacts their likelihood to persist. In contrast, increased social capital—which stems from their development of and participation in personal and professional relationships and networks—can provide much-needed support and resources that help students to overcome the challenges they may face to succeed in their college careers. Such social capital is also important in forming students' new habitus within the college context, or students' mental framework as adapted to the unique environment of the institution. Such adjustment is important as dissonances between students' internal habitus (the habitus they formed during their upbringing) and that of the institution may lead to feelings of isolation, disconnection, and not being able to "fit in" (Lehmann, 2007). As I have established throughout the text, such feelings decrease students' likelihood to persist, pointing to a key area of intervention.

Retention in Practice: Recommendations for Institutions

The following six recommendations serve as a conclusion to this book, and highlight the best practices I believe are most likely to increase student retention in college. Rather than a simple to-do list, these recommendations should be taken together as a starting place for inquiry and program development for higher education institutions seeking to increase their student retention.

1. Understand the student population. It is important to understand the student population of the institution, in order to have a clear picture of the needs and stressors of that population. It is well documented that vulnerable or at-risk students, including first-generation, minority, low socioeconomic status, and nontraditional students as well as students with disabilities (physical and learning) and/or mental health (or other health) issues are more likely to drop out of their studies. As such, the first step in assessing how to improve retention is to understand why the institution's students may be at risk of dropping out, and what their specific needs are. Indeed, in my doctoral study, the findings showed that understanding students is one of the two most important factors influencing student retention. Educators may find that learning about their students by accessing their data helps them to identify students' unique needs better. This knowledge may help educators and the institution more broadly tailor programming to address the specific issues their students face, increasing the efficacy, efficiency, and relevance of retention interventions.

2. Understand the factors impacting student retention. After establishing a clear idea of the student population and their needs, the next step is to consider meaningfully the factors that impact student retention more broadly. The factors are complex and varied. As my study showed, some of the factors that impact student persistence include: the availability and quality of academic support and new student orientation systems, faculty involvement and active communication with students, extracurricular involvement and support, students' goal-setting skills and expectations, and establishing a warm institutional environment during the transition to college. In addition to understanding students as noted above, my research found that establishing strong teacher-student relationships was also one of the two most important factors influencing student retention. These two factors were more important than any other, including students' financial situations or the affordability of college, or the provision of quality services (though they are also important).

3. Support students during their transition to college. The evidence clearly shows that students are most likely to drop out of school during their transition to college. This is due to the high amounts of stress they endure while adjusting to the new demands, social circles, and overall environment of college life. Starting interventions and providing key student support services early on will help to mitigate the challenges students face during this period. This is particularly true for students who may be unprepared or underprepared for college and lack the skills to navigate the social and academic demands of the college environment. Here, providing study and other academic skills training, helping students to set clear and achievable goals, and creating opportunities for personal and professional networking and student engagement may help students to overcome the challenges of the transition period. Additionally, creating a warm institutional environment is important to help students adjust, feel comfortable, and socialize within the college campus—social connection and feelings of belonging play a key role in student persistence.

4. Engage students in the campus. Research has clearly shown the benefits of student engagement in relation to the issue of student retention. Student engagement should occur in both the academic and social life of the institution. In my research, student engagement emerged as the most effective approach or institutional best practice to increase student retention—many participants believed that students' decision to drop out of their program directly resulted from their disengagement with the campus environment. Institutions can increase student engagement in many ways including designing interventions that promote and/or implement extra- or co-curricular cocurricular activities, offer support services, advertise campus activities, use technology to reach the student population, and promote/provide teacher-student and peer mentorship opportunities and relationships.

5. Work together as a unified institution. As noted above, collaboration is a key feature of successful retention programming. Personnel at all levels (e.g., leadership, administration, staff, faculty, support personnel) must work together to develop, implement, and reinforce the messages of retention programming, and to provide support services for students at risk of leaving school. Such support services should include efforts that focus on relationship building between and among staff, faculty, and students, including mentoring and advising programs that last from college entrance until completion. Students are more likely to persist when they feel invested, engaged, and a part of the institution—collaborators in their educational journey. Here, communication between and among faculty, administration, and staff—as well as between staff and students—is of particular import.

6. Provide training and professional development for staff and faculty. Because collaboration is so important in successful retention efforts, all staff must equally understand how and why student retention affects the institution, and what the factors are in students' decision to leave school.

Without the proper training and professional development, staff and/or faculty may lack the skills needed to identify students at risk of leaving school, or to support these students effectively. Providing such training will equip staff with the tools required to participate fully in the institution's retention efforts, while helping them to feel invested in being a part of the solution. It may also make it clear why faculty/staff–student relationships are so important, and help educators to take ownership over the relationship-building process. This will require all members of the institution to work holistically to tackle the pressing issue of student retention in today's higher education environment. A key aspect of training and/or professional development for staff and faculty is faculty empowerment. As my study showed, educators must feel interested and engaged in their teaching, that they are moving forward in their own professional lives. This engagement and empowerment is key to educators' investment in student relationships and how they communicate with students.

References

Ackerman, P. L., Kanfer, R., & Beier, M. E. (2013). Trait complex, cognitive ability, and domain knowledge predictors of baccalaureate success, STEM persistence, and gender differences. *Journal of Educational Psychology, 105*(3), 911–977.

Arendt, J. N. (2013). The effect of public financial aid on dropout from and completion of university education: Evidence from a student grant reform. *Empirical Economics, 44*(3), 1545–1562. doi:10.1007/s00181-012-0638-5

Austin, C. M. (2011). *A model for integrating a career development course program into a college curriculum.* Retrieved from http://gradworks.umi.com/3439796.pdf

Bair, C. R. (1999). *Doctoral students' attrition and persistence: A meta-analysis of research* (Doctoral dissertation). Retrieved from ProQuest Dissertations & Theses Global database. (UMI No. 9917754)

Barrow, L., Brock, T., & Rouse, C. E. (2013). Postsecondary education in the United States: Introducing the issue. *The Future of Children, 23*(1), 3–16.

Bean, J. P., & Metzner, B. S. (1985). A conceptual model of nontraditional undergraduate student attrition. *Review of Educational Research, 55*(4), 485–540. doi:10.3102/00346543055004485

Beasley, M. A., & Fischer, M. J. (2012). Why they leave: The impact of stereotype threat on the attrition of women and minorities from science, math and engineering majors. *Social Psychology of Education, 15,* 427–448. doi:10.1007/s11218-012-9185-3

Beattie, I. R., & Thiele, M. (2016). Connecting in class? College class size and inequality in academic social capital. *The Journal of Higher Education, 87*(3), 332–362. doi:10.1353 /jhe.2016.0017

Belfield, C. R. (2013). Student loans and repayment rates: The role of for-profit colleges. *Research in Higher Education, 54*(1), 1–29. doi:10.1007/s11162-012-9268-1

Bettinger, E. P., Boatman, A., & Long, B. T. (2013). Student supports: Developmental education and other academic programs. *The Future of Children, 23*(1), 93–115.

Boston, W. E., Ice, P., & Gibson, A. M. (2011). Comprehensive assessment of student retention in online learning environments. *Online Journal of Distance Learning Administration, 14*(4). Retrieved from http://www.westga.edu/~distance/ojdla/spring141/boston_ice _gibson141.html

Bourdieu, P. (1986). The forms of capital. In J. Richardson (Ed.). *Handbook of theory and research for the sociology of education* (pp. 241–258). New York, NY: Greenwood.

Bowden, J., & Wood, L. (2011). Sex doesn't matter: The role of gender in the formation of student-university relationships. *Journal of Marketing for Higher Education, 21*, 133–156.

Bowen, W., & Rudenstine, N. (1992). *In pursuit of the Ph.D.* Princeton, NJ: Princeton University Press.

Brand, J. E., & Xie, Y. (2010). Who benefits most from college? Evidence for negative selection in heterogeneous economic returns to higher education. *American Sociological Review, 75*(2), 273–302. doi:10.1177/0003122410363567

Branson, R. A., Marbory, S., Brown, A., Covington, E., McCauley, K., & Nash, A. (2013). A pilot study: An exploration of social, emotional, and academic factors influencing school dropout. *The Researcher, 26,* 1–17.

Brooks, M., Jones, C., & Burt, I. (2013). Are African-American male undergraduate retention programs successful? An evaluation of an undergraduate African-American male retention program. *Journal of African American Studies, 17,* 206–221. doi:10.1007 /s12111-012-9233-2

Byun, S. Y., Irvin, M. J., & Meece, J. L. (2012). Predictors of bachelor's degree completion among rural students at four-year institutions. *Review of Higher Education, 35*(3), 463–484.

Calvert, C. E. (2014). Developing a model and applications for probabilities of student success: A case study of predictive analytics. *Open Learning, 29*(2), 160–173. doi:10.1080 /02680513.2014.931805

Campbell, T. A., & Campbell, D. E. (1997). Faculty/student mentor program: Effects on academic performance and retention. *Research in Higher Education, 38*(6), 727–742.

Cejda, B. D., & Hoover, R. E. (2010). Strategies for faculty-student engagement: How community college faculty engage Latino students. *Journal of College Student Retention: Research, Theory, & Practice, 12*(2), 135–153. doi:10.2190/CS.12.2.b

Carroll, D., Ng, E., & Birch, D. (2013). Strategies to improve retention of postgraduate business students in distance education courses: An Australian case. *Turkish Online Journal of Distance Education, 14*(1), 140–153.

Carnevale, A. P., Rose, S. J., & Hanson, A. R. (2012). Certificates: Gateway to gainful employment and college degrees. *Georgetown University*

Center on Education and the Workforce. Retrieved from http://files.eric. ed.gov/fulltext/ED532679.pdf

Ceci, S. J., Williams, W. M., & Barnett, S. M. (2009). Women's under-representation in science: Sociocultural and biological considerations. *Psychological Bulletin, 135,* 218–261. doi:10.1037/a0014412

Cellini, S. R., & Goldin, C. (2012). *Does federal student aid raise tuition? New evidence on for-profit colleges.* Washington, DC: George Washington University.

Chemers, M. M., Hu, L.-T., & Garcia, B. F. (2001). Academic self-efficacy and first-year college student performance and adjustment. *Journal of Educational Psychology, 93*(1), 55–64. doi:10.1037//0022-0663.93.1.55

Chen, R. (2012). Institutional characteristics and college student dropout risks: A multilevel event history analysis. *Research in Higher Education, 53*(5), 487–505. doi:10.1007 /s11162-011-9241-4

Chen, R., & DesJardins, S. L. (2010). Investigating the impact of financial aid on student dropout risks: Racial and ethnic differences. *The Journal of Higher Education, 81*(2), 179–208.

Colferai Boton, E., & Gregory, S. (2015). Minimizing attrition in online degree courses. *Journal of Educators Online, 12*(1), 62–90. Retrieved from https://www.thejeo.com

Corwin, J. R., & Cintrón, R. (2011). Social networking phenomena in the first-year experience. *Journal of College Teaching & Learning, 8*(1), 25–37. doi:10.19030/tlc.v8i1.983

DeBerard, M. S., Spielman, G. I., & Julka, D. L. (2004). Predictors of academic achievement and retention among college freshmen: A longitudinal study. *College Student Journal, 38,* 66–80.

Deming, D., Goldin, C., & Katz, L. (2012). The for-profit postsecondary school sector: Nimble critters or agile predators? *Journal of Economic Perspectives, 26*(1), 139–164.

Deming, D., Goldin, C., & Katz, L. (2013). For-profit colleges. *The Future of Children, 23*(1), 137–163. doi:10.1353/foc.2013.0005

DesJardins, S. L., Kim, D., & Rzonca, C. S. (2003). A nested analysis of factors affecting bachelor's degree completion. *Journal of College Student Retention, 4,* 407–435.

DesJardins, S. L., & McCall, B. P. (2010). Simulating the effects of financial aid packages on college student stopout, reenrollment spells, and graduation chances. *The Review of Higher Education, 33*(4), 513–541.

DiPrete, T. A., & Buchmann, C. (2006). Gender-specific trends in the value of education and the emerging gender gap in college completion. *Demography, 43*(1), 1–24.

Drake, J. K. (2011). The role of academic advising in student retention and persistence. *About Campus, 16*(3), 8–12.

Dwyer, R. E., Hodson, R., & McCloud, L. (2013). Gender, debt, and dropping out of college. *Gender & Society, 27*(1), 30–55.

Eddy, S. L., Brownell, S. E., & Wenderoth, M. P. (2014). Gender gaps in achievement and participation in multiple introductory biology classrooms. *CBE-Life Sciences Education, 13*(3), 478–492.

Elam, C., Stratton, T., & Gibson, D. D. (2007). Welcoming a new generation to college: The millennial students. *Journal of College Admission, 2007*(195), 20–25. Retrieved from https://www.nacacnet.org/news--publications/publications/journal-of-college-admission

Forsman, J., Linder, C., Moll, R., Fraser, D., & Andersson, S. (2014). A new approach to modeling student retention through an application of complexity thinking. *Studies in Higher Education, 39*(1), 68–86. doi:10.1080/03075079.2011.643298

Foster, D. W. (2008). *Student engagement experiences of African American males at a California community college* (Doctoral dissertation). Available from ProQuest Dissertations and Theses database. (UMI No. 3331201)

Fox, M. F., Sonnert, G., & Nikiforova, I. (2011). Programs for undergraduate women in science and engineering: Issues, problems, and solutions. *Gender & Society, 25*, 589–615.

Gansemer-Topf, A. M., Zhang, Y. L., Beatty, C. C., & Paja, S. (2014). Examining factors influencing attrition at a small, private, selective liberal arts college. *Journal of Student Affairs Research & Practice, 51*(3), 270–285.

Gilardi, S., & Guglielmetti, C. (2011). University life of non-traditional students: Engagement styles and impact on attrition. *The Journal of Higher Education, 82*(1), 33–53. doi:10.1353/jhe.2011.0005

Ginsberg, M., & Wlodkowski, R. (2009). *Diversity and motivation: Culturally responsive teaching* (2nd ed.). San Francisco, CA: Jossey-Bass.

Goldrick-Rab, S., Harris, D. N., & Benson, J. (2011). How need-based financial aid reduces college attrition among low-income public university students: The role of time use. *Society for Research on Educational Effectiveness*, 1–5.

Gooden, S. T., & Martin, K. J. (2014). Facilitating college success among emerging Hispanic serving institutions: Multiple perspectives yield commonly shared diversity goals. *Journal of Public Management & Social Policy, 20*(1), 1–29.

Gurantz, O. (2015). Who loses out? Registration order, course availability, and student behaviors in community college. *Journal of Higher Education, 86*(4), 524–565.

Hagel, P., Horn, A., Owen, S., & Currie, M. (2012). 'How can we help?' The contribution of university libraries to student retention. *Australian Academic & Research Libraries, 43*(3), 214–230.

Heisserer, D. L., & Parette, P. (2002). Advising at-risk students in college and university settings. *College Student Journal, 36*(1), 69–83.

Holliday, M. R. (2015). *First year experience seminars: How contrasting models impact the college transition and retention* (Doctoral dissertation). Retrieved from http://arizona.openrepository.com/arizona/handle/10150/316770

Hout, M. (2012). Social and economic returns to college education in the United States. *Annual Review of Sociology, 38*, 379–400.

Hu, S., McCormick, A. C., & Gonyea, R. M. (2012). Examining the relationship between student learning and persistence. *Innovative Higher Education, 37*(5), 387–395. doi:10.1007/s10755-011-9209-5

Hunt, J., & Eisenberg, D. (2010). Mental health problems and help-seeking behavior among college students. *Journal of Adolescent Health, 46*, 3–10. doi:10.1016/j.jadohealth.2009.08.008

Hurst, C. S., Baranik, L. E., & Daniel, F. (2013). College student stressors: A review of the qualitative research. *Stress & Health, 29*(4), 275–285. doi:10.1002/smi.2465

Jacoby, D. (2006). Effects of part-time faculty employment on community college graduation rates. *The Journal of Higher Education, 77*(6), 1081–1103.

Jaeger, A. J., & Eagan, M. K. (2011). Examining retention and contingent faculty use in a state system of public higher education. *Educational Policy, 25*(3), 507–537. doi:10.1177 /0895904810361723

Jamelske, E. (2008). Measuring the impact of a university first-year experience program on student GPA and retention. *Higher Education, 57*, 373–391. doi:10.1007/s10734-008-9161-1

Jenicke, L. O., Holmes, M. C., & Pisani, M. J. (2013). Approaching the challenge of student retention through the lens of quality control: A conceptual model of university business student retention utilizing Six Sigma. *Journal of College Student Retention: Research, Theory, & Practice, 15*(2), 193–214.

Johnson, D. R., Wasserman, T. H., Yildirim, N., & Yonai, B. A. (2014). Examining the effects of stress and campus climate on the persistence of students of color and white students: An application of Bean and Eaton's psychological model of retention. *Research in Higher Education, 55*(1), 75–100.

Kezar, A., & Eckel, P. (2007). Learning to ensure success of students of color: A systemic approach to effecting change. *Change*, 19–24.

Kolb, M. M. (2005). *The relationship between state appropriations and student retention at public, four-year institutions of higher education* (Unpublished doctoral dissertation). The University of Arizona.

Landek, M. M. (2013). *An examination of commuter and residential student time allocation and relationship to student retention* (Doctoral dissertation). http://hdl.handle.net/10027/9991

Lansing, P., & Olsen, D. S. (2011). The (subsidized) business of higher education: An ethical analysis of the federal funding in for-profit higher education. *Mustang Journal of Accounting & Finance, 1*, 118–135.

Leeds, E., Campbell, S., Baker, H., Ali, R., Brawley, D., & Crisp, J. (2013). The impact of student retention strategies: An empirical study. *International Journal of Management in Education, 7*(1), 22–43.

Lehmann, W. (2007). "I just didn't feel like I fit in": The role of habitus in university dropout decisions. *Canadian Journal of Higher Education, 37*(2), 89–110. Retrieved from http://journals.sfu.ca/cjhe/index.php/cjhe/index

Lei, S. A. (2015). Variation in study patterns among college students: A review of literature. *College Student Journal, 49*(2), 195–198.

Lemp, P. H. (1980). Determinants of persistence in graduate education: The doctoral student. *Dissertation Abstracts International, 41*, 05A.

Lillibridge, F. (2008). Retention tracking using institutional data. *New Directions of Community College*, 19–30. doi:10.1002/cc.332

Lin, S.-P. (2015). Using EDM for developing EWS to predict university students drop out. *International Journal of Intelligent Technologies and Applied Statistics, 8*(4), 365–388. doi:10.6148/IJITAS.2015.0804.05

Lin, T. C., Yu, W. W. C., & Chen, Y. C. (2012). Determinants and probability prediction of college student retention: New evidence from the Probit model. *International Journal of Education Economics & Development, 3*(3), 217–236.

Lobosco, K. (2016, October 18). Students are graduating with $30,000 in student loans. *CNN Money*. Retrieved from http://money.cnn.com/2016/10/18/pf/college/average-student-loan-debt/index.html

Lowery, J. W. (2004). Student affairs for a new generation. *New Directions for Student Services, 2004*(106), 87–99. doi:10.1002/ss.127

Mandracchia, J. T., & Pendleton, S. (2015). Understanding college students' problems: Dysfunctional thinking, mental health, and maladaptive behavior. *Journal of College Student Retention: Research, Theory and Practice, 17*(2), 226–242. doi:10.1177 /1521025115578235

Mangold, W. D., Bean, L. G., Adams, D. J., Schwab, W. A., & Lynch, S. M. (2002). Who goes who stay: An assessment of the effect of a freshman mentoring and unit registration program on college retention. *Journal College Student Retention, 4*(2), 95–122.

McCarthy, P. R., & McCarthy, H. M. (2006). When case studies are not enough: Integrating experiential learning into business curricula. *Journal of Education for Business, 81*(4), 201–204. doi:10.3200/JOEB.81.4.201-204

Melguizo, T., Torres, F. S., & Jaime, H. (2011). The association between financial aid availability and the college dropout rates in Colombia. *Higher Education, 62*(2), 231–247.

Merianos, A. L., Nabors, L. A., Vidourek, R. A., & King, K. A. (2013). The impact of self-esteem and social support on college students' mental health. *American Journal of Health Studies, 28*(1), 27–34.

Mitchel, M. J. (2003). Resource allocation through the lens of student attrition. *Independent School Magazine, 63*(4), 55–60. Retrieved from www.independentschoolsmagazine.co.uk

Morgan, M. (Ed.). (2013). *Improving the student experience: A practical guide for universities and colleges.* London, United Kingdom: Routledge.

Moosai, S., Walker, D. A., & Floyd, D. L. (2011). Using student and institutional characteristics to predict graduation rates at community colleges: New developments in performance measures and institutional effectiveness. *Community College Journal of Research & Practice, 35*(10), 802–816.

Mulryan-Kyne, C. (2010). Teaching large classes at college and university level: Challenges and opportunities. *Teaching in Higher Education, 15*(2), 175–185.

National Commission on Higher Education Attainment. (2013). *An open letter to college and university leaders: College completion must be our priority.* Retrieved from http://www.acenet.edu/news-room/Pages/An-Open-Letter-to-College-and-University-Leaders.aspx

Needham, G., Nurse, R., Parker, J., Scantlebury, N., & Dick, S. (2013). Can an excellent distance learning library service support student retention and how can we find out? *Open Learning: The Journal of Open, Distance, & e-Learning, 28*(2), 135–140.

Nelson, L. (2014, July 30). 7 charts that show what happened to 31 million American college dropouts. *Vox.* Retrieved from http://www.vox.com/2014/7/30/5949139/americas-31-million-college-dropouts-in-7-charts

Nichols, M. (2010). Student perceptions of support services and the influence of targeted interventions on retention in distance education. *Distance Education, 31*(1), 93–113. doi:10.1080/01587911003725048

Niu, S. X., & Tienda, M. (2013). High school economic composition and college persistence. *Research in Higher Education, 54*(1), 30–62. doi:10.1007/s11162-012-9265-4

Nordstrom, A. H., Goguen, L. M. S., & Hiester, M. (2014). The effect of social anxiety and self-esteem on college adjustment, academics, and retention. *Journal of College Counseling, 17*(1), 48–63. doi:10.1002/j.2161-1882.2014.00047.x

O'Keeffe, P. (2013). A sense of belonging: Improving student retention. *College Student Journal, 47*(4), 605–613. Retrieved from http://www.projectinnovation.com/college-student-journal.html

Papamitsiou, Z., & Economides, A. (2014). Learning analytics and educational data mining in practice: A systematic literature review of empirical evidence. *Educational Technology & Society, 17*(4), 49–64. Retrieved from http://www.ifets.info

Pascarella, E. T., Duby, P. B., & Iverson, B. K. (1983). A test and reconceptualization of a theoretical model of college withdrawal in a commuter institution setting. *Sociology of Education, 56,* 88–100. Retrieved from http://www.jstor.org/discover/10.2307/2112657?uid=3738824&uid=2&uid=4&sid=21104622800573

Paulsen, M. B., & St. John, E. P. (2002). Social class and college costs: Examining the financial nexus between college choice and persistence. *The Journal of Higher Education, 73*(2), 189–235. doi:10.1353/jhe.2002.0023

Presley, C. L. (1996). Individual and institutional factors that affect the success of African-American graduate and professional school students. *Dissertation Abstracts International, 56,* 08A.

Pusser, B., Breneman, D. W., Gansneder, B. M., Kohl, K. J., Levin, J. S., Milam, J. H., & Turner, S. E. (2007). *Returning to learning: Adults' success in college is key to America's future.* Retrieved from https://www.luminafoundation.org/files/publications/ReturntolearningApril2007.pdf

Redman Mingo, V. A. (2010). *The relationships among student characteristic variables, student engagement variables, and the academic performance of African American male students at two-year colleges* (Doctoral dissertation). Retrieved from ProQuest Dissertations & Theses Global database. (UMI No. 3402824)

Reyes, J. A. (2015). The skinny on big data in education: Learning analytics simplified. *TechTrends, 59*(2), 75–80. doi:10.1007/s11528-015-0842-1

Robbins, S. B., Oh, I., Le, H., & Button, C. (2009). Intervention effects on college performance and retention as mediated by motivational, emotional, and social control factors: Integrated meta-analytic path analyses. *Journal of Applied Psychology, 94*(5), 1163–1184. doi:10.1037/a0015738

Ross-Gordon, J. M. (2011). Research on adult learners: Supporting the needs of a student population that is no longer nontraditional. *Peer Review, 13*(1), 26–29. Retrieved from http://www.aacu.org/peerreview

Rovai, A. P., & Downey, J. R. (2010). Why some distance education programs fail while others succeed in a global environment. *The Internet & Higher Education, 13*(3), 141–147.

Rubin, B. (2013). University business models and online practices: A third way. *Online Journal of Distance Learning Administration, 15*(1). Retrieved from http://www.westga.edu /~distance/ojdla/spring161/rubin.html

Ryan, R. M., & Deci, E. L. (2000). Intrinsic and extrinsic motivations: Classic definitions and new directions. *Contemporary Educational Psychology, 25,* 54–67. doi:10.1006/ceps.1999.1020

Sgro, A. H. (2006). *The perception of parents of the appropriate degree of parental involvement in an independent boarding school: A matter of trust*

(Doctoral dissertation). Available from ProQuest Dissertations and Theses database. (UMI No.3210005)

Sibson, K., Gregory, D. E., & Kurisky, B. P. D. (2014). Retention issues of mature students: A comparative higher education analysis of programs in the United States and Ireland. *Journal of Counselling & Development in Higher Education Southern Africa, 1,* 59–76.

Sladek, A. (2014). Constructing the crisis: Audience perceptions of for-profit education and institutional integrity in the closure of Dana College. *International Journal for Educational Integrity, 10*(2), 60–71.

Smart, J. (2010). Differential patterns of change and stability in student learning outcomes in Holland's academic environments: The role of environmental consistency. *Research in Higher Education, 51*(5), 468–482. doi:10.1007/s11162-010-9163-6

Sontam, V., & Gabriel, G. (2012). Student engagement at a large suburban community college: Gender and race differences. *Community College Journal of Research & Practice, 36*(10), 808–820.

Sparks, P. J., & Nuñez, A. M. (2014). The role of postsecondary institutional urbanicity in college persistence. *Journal of Research in Rural Education, 29*(6), 1–19.

St. John, E. P., Paulsen, M. B., & Carter, D. F. (2005). Diversity, college costs and postsecondary opportunity: An examination of the financial nexus between college choice and persistence for African Americans and Whites. *The Journal of Higher Education, 76,* 545–569.

Stebleton, M. J., Soria, K. M., & Huesman, R. L. (2014). First-generation students' sense of belonging, mental health, and use of counseling services at public research universities. *Journal of College Counseling, 17*(1), 6–20. doi:10.1002/j.2161-1882.2014.00044.x

Stoessel, K., Ihme, T. A., Barbarino, M.-L., Fisseler, B., & Stürmer, S. (2015). Sociodemographic diversity and distance education: Who drops out from academic programs and why? *Research in Higher Education, 56,* 228–246. doi:10.1007/s11162-014-9343-x

Street, H. D. (2010). Factors influencing a learner's decision to drop-out or persist in higher education distance learning. *Online Journal of Distance Learning Administration, 13*(4).

Swecker, H. K., Fifolt, M., & Searby, L. (2013). Academic advising and first-generation college students: A quantitative study on student retention. *NACADA Journal, 33*(1), 46–53. http://dx.doi.org/10.12930/NACADA-13-192

Sykes, R. P. (1996). *Staying power: Independent schools and retention* (Doctoral dissertation). Available from ProQuest Dissertations and Theses database. (UMI No.9701360)

Tan-Wilson, A., & Stamp, N. (2015). College students' view of work–life balance in STEM research careers: Addressing negative preconceptions. *CBE – Life Sciences Education, 14,* 1–13. doi:10.1187/cbe.14-11-0210

Tinto, V. (1993). *Leaving college: Rethinking the causes and cures of student attrition.* Chicago, IL: University of Chicago Press.

Terrell, S. R., Snyder, M. M., Dringus, L. P., & Maddrey, E. (2012). A grounded theory of connectivity and persistence in a limited residency doctoral program. *The Qualitative Report, 17,* 1–14. Retrieved from http://www.nova.edu/ssss/QR/QR17/terrell.pdf

Tuckman, B. W., & Kennedy, G. J. (2011). Teaching learning strategies to increase success of first-term college students. *Journal of Experimental Education, 79*(4), 478–504. doi:10.1080/00220973.2010.512318

Turner, P., & Thompson, E. (2014). College retention initiatives meeting the needs of millennial freshman students. *College Student Journal, 48*(1), 94–104. Retrieved from http://www.projectinnovation.com/college-student-journal.html

U.S. Department of Education, National Center for Education Statistics. (2002). *The condition of education 2002* (NCES 2002–025). Retrieved from nces.ed.gov/pubs2002/2002025.pdf

Veenstra, C. P. (2009). A strategy for improving freshman college retention. *Journal for Quality & Participation, 31*(4), 19–23. Retrieved from www.asq.org/pub/jqp

Verbert, K., Manouselis, N., Drachsler, H., & Duval, E. (2012). Dataset-driven research to support learning and knowledge analytics. *Educational Technology & Society, 15*(3), 133–148. Retrieved from http://www.ifets.info

Walters, E. W., & McKay, S. (2005). Strategic planning and retention within the community college setting. *College Student Affairs Journal, 25*(1), 50–63. doi:1014585561

Wang, X., Liu, C., Zhang, L., Yue, A., Shi, Y., Chu, J., & Rozelle, S. (2013). Does financial aid help poor students succeed in college? *China Economic Review, 25*, 27–43.

Weiss, C. C., Carolan, B. V., & Baker-Smith, E. C. (2010). Big school, small school: (Re)testing assumptions about high school size, school engagement and mathematics achievement. *Journal of Youth & Adolescence, 39*(2), 163–176. doi:10.1007/s10964-009-9402-3

Willcoxson, L., Cotter, J., & Joy, S. (2011). Beyond the first-year experience: The impact on attrition of student experiences throughout undergraduate degree studies in six diverse universities. *Studies in Higher Education, 36*(3), 331–352. doi:10.1080/03075070903581533

Wilson, R. (2010). For-profit colleges change higher education's landscape. *The Chronicle of Higher Education, 56*(22), 1–19.

Windham, M. H., Rehfuss, M. C., Williams, C. R., Pugh, J. V., & Tincher-Ladner, L. (2014). Retention of first-year community college students. *Community College Journal of Research & Practice, 38*, 1–12. doi:10.1080/10668926.2012.743867

Witting, P. A. (n.d.). *Student motivation and retention: Strategic and tactical responses*. Retrieved from http://www.hull.ac.uk/engprogress/

Prog1Papers/Witting%20Glamorgan.pdf

Yang, C.-C., & Brown, B. B. (2015). Factors involved in associations between Facebook use and college adjustment: Social competence, perceived usefulness, and use patterns. *Computers in Human Behavior, 46*, 245–253. doi:10.1016/j.chb.2015.01.015

Yasmin, D. (2013). Application of the classification tree model in predicting learner dropout behaviour in open and distance learning. *Distance Education, 34*(2), 218–231. doi:10.1080/01587919.2013.793642

Yu, C. H., DiGangi, S., Jannasch-Pennell, A., & Kaprolet, C. (2010). A data mining approach for identifying predictors of student retention from sophomore to junior year. *Journal of Data Science, 8,* 307–325. Retrieved from http://ww.w.creative-wisdom.com/pub/mirror /JDS-574.pdf

Yu, H. (2014). The effect of part-time faculty on student degree or certificate completion in two-year community colleges. *Journal of Collective Bargaining in the Academy, 9,* 1–23.

Yu, K., & Ertl, H. (2014). For-profit colleges in the economic crisis: Thriving in tough times? *International Research in Education, 2*(1), 118–133.

Zaddach, C. W. (2013). *Beyond retention: Exploring mental health benefits of living learning programs* (Doctoral dissertation). Retrieved from http://ecommons.luc.edu/luc_diss/1121/

Zwick, R. (1991). *Differences in graduate school attainment patterns across academic programs and demographic groups.* Princeton, NJ: Educational Testing Service.

www.ingramcontent.com/pod-product-compliance
Lightning Source LLC
Chambersburg PA
CBHW071850230426
43671CB00012B/2134